To Mom:

I THOUGHT YOU WOULD
ENJOY THIS. I HEARED
ABOUT IT ON NPR
A FEW MONTHS AGO.
MERRY CHRISTMAS!
LOVE
DAUGHTER #1 Kim CBrett

SARA, JESS, JOE
& OF COURSE
Ian

Received
December
27th 2005

Poplollies & Bellibones

A CELEBRATION OF LOST WORDS

ALONG WITH

Tenderfeet & Ladyfingers

A COMPENDIUM OF BODY LANGUAGE

Poplollies & Bellibones

A CELEBRATION OF LOST WORDS

ALONG WITH

Tenderfeet & Ladyfingers

A COMPENDIUM OF BODY LANGUAGE

Susan Kelz Sperling

FOREWORD BY WILLARD R. ESPY

KONECKY&KONECKY

In memory of Boris Burac

Aimcrier

Contents

Foreword

For several years I have kept an eye peeled for an authoritative necrology of words presumed dead. *Poplollies and Bellibones* is clearly (though in embryo, which seems odd for a necrology) the book I was waiting for. It will doubtless proceed through edition after edition, each more comprehensive than the last in vocabulary, more specific in category, more detailed in etymology. It will grow vaster—though, one hopes, less slowly—than Andrew Marvell's empires.

But let the future take care of itself. In the book as it stands, Susan Kelz Sperling has rendered a signal service. She has given us a gorgeous entertainment, redolent with smiles and chuckles for anyone who believes that words are complex beings and that sometimes it pleases them to amuse as they communicate. *Poplollies* will astonish you. It will divert you. It will instruct you. It will whet your appetite for more.

By way of starters, the author has lined up perhaps four hundred usages that were once familiar but are now forgotten. She has arranged them as if her book were a museum of natural history—in a series of dioramas, where each word is posed like a stuffed animal against a replica of its habitat, looking as if alive. A series of rounds (called garlands by the British poet Alastair Reid, originator of the form) leads the reader from one defunct word to the next, explaining each along the way until he is returned at last, exhausted but triumphant, to the place where he started. Playlets, verses, and dialogues similarly define and establish the author's poplollies in the context of their time.

There is a paradox here. Ms. Sperling reminds us that any word still in print still lives, be it available only in the most arcane lexicons and there stigmatized as obsolete, archaic, rare, dialectal, slang, or vulgar. Some of the specimens in her museum may well thrive to this day in remote hamlets of England, Scotland, Ireland, and Wales.

Even on this side of the Atlantic, a few of Ms. Sperling's choices—*widdershins* and *welkin,* for instance—remain recognizable. To be sure, they seldom appear in everyday conversation; now that witches are back in style, *widdershins* would be more likely to show up at a coven than at a cocktail party.

I spoke in my opening sentence of words presumed dead. The caveat was important. Even after being embalmed by linguists and formally laid out in their coffins for interment, words have a way of sitting up, calling for a sip of water to restore their strength, and returning as lively as ten-year-old children to their verbal rounds. *Snollygoster,* for instance, first recorded about 1865, soon went out of use again, only to be revived by President Harry S Truman, who defined it as "a man born out of wedlock." He was promptly called to account by linguistic pundits, who declared the original meaning was "shyster." However defined, *snollygoster* is back in circulation.

One cadaver memorialized in this book seems to have missed its chance at just such a triumphant return. I refer to *acersecomic,* "one whose hair is never cut." In the 1960s, when hair cascaded to the hips on male and female alike to symbolize disaffection, *acersecomic* was ripe for a second coming. Even now it must stir fretfully in its grave.

We are well rid of *floccinaucinihilipilification*, "the habit of belittling," reported here as a linkage of words from an Eton grammar of Latin. Surely this monster can never have entered the vernacular— except perhaps as a joke, like *supercalifragilisticexpialidocious,* * popularized by Walt Disney in a motion picture a few years back.

But if it would do any good, I would gladly give mouth-to-mouth resuscitation to *chantpleure,* a chiaroscuric doublet from the French meaning to sing and weep at the same time. A lovely word.

It appears that the British began very early on to transform proper names into common nouns. (They are still at it.) *Kidcote,* once generic for "prison," was named for a prison in York. A fabric from Ormuz, a city near the entrance to the Persian Gulf, was promptly termed *ormuzine.* A coarse woolen cloth called *penistone* was woven in the town of that name.

Since the author has confined herself to words that flourished hundreds of years ago in the British Isles (few in this book were born later than the seventeenth century), she has not yet had to face the dilemma of nonce terms. But if she adds to her collection, she must deal with them sooner or later. A word that was never really extant can scarcely be listed as extinct. How long must it persist before it becomes more than a passing aberration and at death is entitled to funerary rites?

* A correspondent reports hearing the word as early as 1926. It probably originated still earlier.

Nonce means "temporary; for the moment." The second edition of *Webster's Unabridged Dictionary* gives three examples of nonce words: *diphrelatic, decorist,* and *mammonolatry.* (Philosophers, economists, and sociologists must find themselves regularly reinventing *mammonolatry,* surely the most pervasive and enduring of America's heretic religions.)

The American Heritage Dictionary mentions but one nonce word, *mileconsuming,* used by William Faulkner in "the wagon beginning to fall into its slow and mileconsuming clatter." Dictionaries treat nonces as the work of individuals—neologisms that failed. Yet many of them spring up simultaneously and unbidden, like dandelions, through some acidifying or alkalizing of the social soil. They last until the soil changes again, and then disappear. In my childhood, *catsup,* a trade name for "ketchup," was considered, in our family, the preferred usage; yet I have not heard anyone say *catsup* for twenty years.

When Ms. Sperling shifts her sights from Britain to America, what will she do about such feisty offspring of Jacksonian democracy as *absquatulate* ("to depart stealthily"), *obflisticate* ("to obliterate"), or *ramsquaddle* ("to beat")? Each fluttered about for an hour, like a mayfly, and then perished. Should they be considered obsolete, or simply nonwords? They were born on the wrong side of the blanket, to be sure, but so were other demonic products that have survived colloquially: *bodacious, rip-roaring, rip-snorter, teetotaler, hornswoggle, shebang, shindig, skedaddle, splendiferous, spondulicks, slumgullion.*

And when did the dead words die? The vital statistics on births are mostly available, give or take a hundred years. Today we have grown comparatively precise in our dating, partly because the underground streams in which new words, especially those involving alienation, so commonly hatch; that is to say, the underworld and the counterculture are closer to the surface than they once dared be. As soon as a new locution emerges to cock a snook at society, *Time* or the *Reader's Digest* leaps on it with a glad cry and flings it into the central current of the language. But it is more difficult to be certain when a doddering word slips from public ken. It generally lingers in old reference works, sometimes with a note of the year it was first sighted:

> *Hoddypeak,* n. Simpleton, blockhead (1505)

How much more satisfactory if the reference encompassed the word's entire life span!

> *Hoddypeak,* n. Simpleton, blockhead (1505–1733)

Perhaps Ms. Sperling will explore dates of obsoletion in her next edition.

Perhaps, too, she will uncover more of the words' life stories. The origins she does mention are as bemusing as the words themselves. To think that her titular *bellibones*, scarcely aesthetic appearing at a glance, actually means "a lovely lady, a pretty lass," and is a hobson-jobson from French *belle et bonne*, "beautiful and good"! That epiphany alone would be enough to justify this book.

Never again, alas, will we hear a crane *crunkle*, a sheep *blore*, or a donkey *winx*. Never again will we see a *shiterow* flap along a stream, though herons may abound. Nor shall I ever, however great the provocation, dare call one of my sons-in-law an *odam,* with the accent on the last syllable.

The author's device of displaying obsolete words in their original settings so intrigued me that I could not resist trying the trick myself. The result is the following *chant royal.* The theme and treatment are limited by the vocabulary at my disposal; you will find all the unfamiliar terms defined in the glossary. If you are sometimes doubtful about the pronunciation, why, so was I; simply arrange the sound of each word to fit it into the meter of the line.

CHANTPLEURE

Thought I to me, "A chant royal I'll dite—
Make much ado of words long laid away—
Wake eldnyng from bards resigned to cite
The sloomy phrases of Min Cheever's day.
I'll chantpleure, though I compass but a page;
I'll man illume, from April bud till snow,
In song all merry-go-sorry, con and pro."
I would have pulled it off, too, given time,
Had not a hidden ha-ha stubbed my toe:
Words obsolete are mighty hard to rhyme.

Ah, hadivist, in younghede, when from night
There dawned abluscent a fair morn in May
(The word for dawning, sparrow-fart, won't quite
Fit in here)—hadivist, I say,
That I'd in chair day by stoop-gallant age
Be shabbed, adushed, pitchkettled, suggilled so,
Would I have been more hoful? Yes . . . or no.
One scantling bit of outwit's all that I'm

Quite sure of, after years of catch-and-throw:
Words obsolete are mighty hard to rhyme.

In younghede, ne'er a thrip gave I for blight
Of cark or ribble—I was ycore, gay;
From hum to hum boonfellows vied, each wight
By t'others aimcried, till as one we'd sway,
Turngiddy. Blashy beer could not assuage
Such thirst, nor kill-priest, even.
$\qquad\qquad\qquad\qquad$ No Lothario
Outdid my eaubruche on Poplolly Row.
The fairhead who eyebit me in my prime
Soon knew my donge. (The meaning's clear, although
Words obsolete are mighty hard to rhyme.)

Pert daggle-tails first faged my appetite;
No inwit saved me from their shittle play.
Bedswerver, likewise housebreak, was I hight—
"Poop-noddy at poop-noddy."
$\qquad\qquad\qquad\qquad$ Now I pray
That other fonkins reach safe anchorage—
Find bellibone, as I did, to bestrow
The lip-clap seeds that into true-head grow;
So strewn, we fellowfeel, and scrow-ward climb.
(Frush mubblefubbles. My own climb was slow:
Words obsolete are mighty hard to rhyme.)

Now on the wong at cock-shut fails the light;
Birds' sleepy croodles cease. Not long to stay
Once nesh as open-tide, I now affright—
Am lennow, spittle-ready—samded clay,
A clutched bell-penny my remaining wage.
I wait, acclumsid. No more toward the scrow

I mount. Downsteepy is the pit below.
Ah, hadivist . . . a drumly, trantled chime.
My very outwit is malapropos:
Words obsolete are mighty hard to rhyme.

Envoy

The ghosts of blore and paggle past me blow—
The coverslut, the okselle, are *de trop*.
To lose straight-fingered phrases seems a crime.
Yet in my heart I cry, "Bravissimo!"—
Words obsolete are mighty hard to rhyme.

My analogies in the foregoing paragraphs have generally referred to the animal kingdom. Overall, however, the comparison of obsolete words with flora may be more appropriate. Turn the page, now, and sniff the fragrance of some of the most aromatic flowers that ever faded in a British garden. This is how they were in their prime. Pluck your favorites, as I have plucked mine, and offer them as a tuzzy-muzzy to Susan Kelz Sperling.

—WILLARD R. ESPY

Part 1

Poplollies & Bellibones

A CELEBRATION OF LOST WORDS

Word collecting is a chronic illness, a pleasurable malady but nonetheless impossible to cure. My first recollection of loving words for their own sake comes from the fifth grade, when the teacher subjected a friend of mine to peer ridicule for having written in a composition, "Mrs. Adams has pail blue eyes." His homophonic error made me thrill at the thought of seeing the eyes of this teacher, whom I disliked, floating helplessly in a bucket. My next symptomatic memory is of an impatient classmate, eager to break into a long line for lunch, asking me, "Where can I get ahead?"

By the eighth grade I realized that playing with words was more than a hobby. In the twelfth grade I exchanged colorful, pun-filled words with the kindred soul and teacher whose wit, whose love for language, and whose encouragement were to direct the course of my life. The writing of this book is therefore somewhat his fault; the publication of it is my eulogy to him.

Undoubtedly, my addiction/affliction is the unforeseen genetic gift of a mother and father whose native tongue was not English and who, coming from Europe, incorporated the fine and delicious subtleties of their other languages into what became their own refined patterns. Hearing other languages spoken at home by both them and my linguistically talented older sister made me aware very early of how words combine to communicate meaning. The generosity of unnamed fellow-feeling friends, professors, and former students is imprinted in these pages. The special patience and loving perseverance of a very good man and discerner of words, my husband, made this book possible. The spark of response to wordplay that my three children already exhibit is reinforcement that I had not counted on and proof that this pun-ishing chronic illness is either happily hereditary or at best contagious. You, the reader, will remain exposed to infection if you continue to ingest these pages. For the sake of the future of the English language, read on; don't quarantine yourselves. Spread the germs and let them multiply so that our disease will itself become the cure for today's sterile syntax and senseless wagging of the tongue.

Introduction

Since the dawn of language, words have been going through a process of natural selection in which only the most fit survive. Every one of us, as a reader, writer, and speaker, shapes the course of language by choosing the words we want to convey our message and rejecting those we deem inappropriate in one context or another. In short, we place value judgments on words. If this complex process of selection is multiplied by billions of people over thousands of years, it becomes apparent that language goes through an evolutionary process of its own.

All the words that are used in different ways in this book are referred to as obsolete, rare, or dialect in the various dictionaries and are seldom or never used today in writing or speech. Why, then, resurrect these words? Like an irreplaceable antique, a little-known or redis-covered word can not only be a source of pleasure in itself but may also open up fascinating insights into the past. One must not infer that because a word died, it deserved never to have lived. The sounds and meanings of these colorful dead words evoke a very alive past when these words that sound strange to us were communication tools for the people living then. Over the course of time customs changed and words associated with them fell out of use. Through this process of addition and subtraction our language evolved.

The evolution of the English language is usually divided into three major periods: Old English, from around A.D. 450 to 1150; Middle English, from around 1150 to 1500, and Modern English, from 1500 on. Invasions, wars, shifts in population, and changing lifestyles all effected changes in our language. As early as 500 B.C., Celtic invaders from the European mainland peopled the area we know now as the British Isles until more powerful Roman armies, beginning with Julius Caesar's in 55 B.C., began their conquest in search of mineral wealth and land. Over the centuries, other groups of invaders, the Irish, the Picts from Scotland, the Teutonic tribes—Saxons, Angles, Jutes, Frisians—and the Danes all left their mark on the language. In 1066, with William the Conqueror's victory over England, the heavily Germanic amalgam known as Anglo-Saxon or Old English took on French overtones and England was thrust into a new era of language consciousness.

The Renaissance of the sixteenth century, that marvelous turning point in the history of Europe, had a great impact on the English language. Travel to new lands, the rounding of the Cape of Good Hope, expeditions to the Far East, and the settling of America contributed to the exchange of ideas and a resulting influx of words into the English lexicon, as well as to the spread of English to faraway places. When the Church of England wielded its power over Catholicism during the Reformation, medieval Latin scholarship as embodied in monastic thought gave way to English. Translations of classical literature from Latin and Greek into English revived interest in words from those languages. Finally, the newly invented printing press standardized English and spread it far and wide.

The age of Elizabeth I, the true English Renaissance, epitomizes an intoxication with the arts. Word fever spread throughout the land as Elizabethan writers revived old words, coined new ones, and created the masterpieces that we moderns recognize as the body of great English literature. Shakespeare and his contemporaries played with language for the sheer pleasure of it. Their gamesmanship with words often meant using as many synonyms as one could find for one word. In the flowery 1600s a total of twenty-one words were synonyms for the "lowly" literary device we call a pun or a play on words: *bull, carriwitchet, clench, clinch, crotchet, figary, flam, jerk, liripoop, paronomasia, pundigrion, quarterquibble, quibble, quiblin, quiddity, quillet, quip, quirk, sham, whiblin,* and *whim.* A favorite pastime involved conjuring up new words by stringing together existing ones. Sometimes these inventions were exaggeratedly wind filled, as is the case with *floccinaucinihilipilification,* a word that may have been invented as a parody of its literal meaning, the habit of judging even important things as worthless.

Florid flights into verbosity went unrestrained until the eighteenth century, when academic societies during the Age of Reason met to determine taste in language. The rules of grammar and syntax were never so respected as during that time when formality, polite manners, and self-control were *de rigueur.* Purists censored words they deemed improper to use in public and others that happened to sound suspicious. Later, Romanticists rejoined with their metaphors and other figures of speech, proving that language, like other arts, mirrors the mood of the times.

We see in the twentieth century, with its fast pace and cry for incessant change, a direction toward economy in speech. Definite rules preclude casual spelling and pronunciation. Exacting people nowadays want the exact word in its exact place to get the message across with brevity and immediacy, even at the expense of grammar and originality. But word fanciers still abound.

Many of the words found herein have passed out of use because the obsolete customs, beliefs, and objects they described changed or were superseded by others. They were not universal terms, for they specifically applied only to their time.

Gone are the days of magic and health cures when a *zopissa,* a poultice of wax and pitch, would have soothed one with *agrum,* a profound swelling of the cheeks and mouth. We have come a long way from threatening naughty children with a *mumpoker* to frighten them and drive out their evil spirits. When they interrupt, we don't say, "Stop coming in with your five eggs." Fashion has forgotten the fabric *ormuzine,* once a desirable import from the Persian Gulf, and the extravagant *zendalet,* a shawl worn by Venetian women, no longer drapes over the sides of gondolas. An actor may still *blore,* bray, or bleat like an animal, and *crunkle,* cry like a crane, thereby overdoing his part, but we no longer call him a *tearcat* for his dramatic excesses.

We can rejoice that we are no longer subject to the

lovecup, a local market tax, the *swarf-penny*, money due to a castle guard when his period of service was terminated, and the *shongable*, a tax one paid for having a certain kind of shoes made. But today we could certainly benefit from the services of a *streetman*, an official appointed to oversee good government of London streets. A further loss to society is that obsolete custom of setting aside special days as *love days*, when parties were ordered by law to settle their difficulties through amicable arbitration, perhaps with the help of an *oddwoman*, the precursor of today's ombudsman.

Most by-gone punishments are best not revived, but the few to be mentioned here are too imaginative to be left in oblivion. The Old English practice called *corsned*, ordeal by exorcised bread, was the easiest of three medieval tests a prisoner underwent to determine his guilt or innocence. It called for the accused to swallow what he knew might be his last bite of food, an ounce of cheese or bread consecrated with a form of exorcism by a priest. If the morsel caused the person to become pale and go into convulsions he was deemed guilty, but if he maintained his health he was considered innocent. More horrible was the ordeal by fire, in which the prisoner was declared innocent only if a red-hot iron did not burn him. Equally severe was the ordeal by water, during which the person was bound and thrown into the water and pronounced innocent only if he sank without returning to the surface. It is hoped that the victim was retrieved in time to be exonerated.

A complement to the pillory on the village green was the *cucking-stool*. The offender, guilty of fairly harmless acts such as disorderly conduct or unfair trading practices, was fastened to a chair and jeered at by the general public or carried to a pond and dunked.

The most inventive punishment of all was the form of public derision popular through the late 1800s in parts of England, Scotland and Wales called *riding the stang*. It consisted of a procession in which an unfaithful husband was carried atop a ladder through village streets for women to censure, verbally or otherwise, at certain points along the route. A man who had beaten his wife was subjected to a slightly different mode of public ridicule. For three nights, trumpeters would rouse the villagers to join a parade, sometimes including the offender, in which the wittiest man of the town, seated in a chair strapped to poles, would be carried aloft, to the clanging of pots, pans, and horns. The mounted orator would periodically stop to proclaim a verse, such as this one recalled by William Andrews in *Old-Time Punishments:*

Here we come with a ran, dan, dang:
It's not for you, nor for me, we ride this stang;
But for——, whose wife he did bang.

Another embellishment on the practice involved burning effigies of the offenders on the village green or in front of their houses. In the ritual called *skimmington*, two performers, impersonating the husband and wife, rode through the town in a donkey cart beating each other with a ladle and skimmer, hence the name *skimmington*. They put on an especially animated performance in front of the victims' house.

Perhaps the aforementioned guilty husband had met his mistress on the havoc-filled day that people in Lancashire celebrated in the 1880s, namely *Lifting Monday*. On the Monday following Easter it was the ritual for men to lift up and kiss every woman they met. According to custom, women would reciprocate by doing likewise on Easter Tuesday, but our sources are incomplete as to whether women actually tried to lift the men. Perhaps their mutual attempt at lifting, which starts with an embrace, turned the custom into a hug. Unfortunately, these practices were short-lived because of the disturbances they caused. Some customs and the words that accompanied them are indeed better left in the dead past, but this one would be a gem to resurrect, if only for one day.

In contrast to the many obsolete words with modern synonyms, there are a number of dead words for which we have no modern equivalents, even though the obsolete words expressed timeless sentiments. What is indeed so special about these words is that they sum up in just a few syllables the eternal feelings that one often struggles at great length to find the right words for today. For example, to *chantpleure*, obviously a French contribution to our language, meant to sing and cry at the same time, perhaps at hearing a *merry-go-sorry*, a wonderful term for the kind of experience that elicits simultaneous feelings of joy and sorrow. Like the popular jokes that begin, "I have good news and bad news," a writer named Nicholas Breton wrote in 1606 in *Chance, Chance*, "Thou has told me of such a merry-go-sorry, as I have not often heard of: I am sorry for thy ill fortune, but am glad to see thee alive." Similar in spirit is the adjective *agathokakological*, a Greek term that meant possessing a combination of good and evil. Also of Greek origin are two other words lacking one-word modern equivalents, *xenodochial*, hospitable to strangers, and *philotimy*, love of honor. The singular word *storge* ("store-gee") meant the kind of love a parent would naturally feel for his children, as Thackeray used it in *Pendennis* in 1850: "I could have . . . adored in her the Divine beneficence in endowing us with the maternal storge, which . . . sanctifies the history of mankind."

Many old words describe that melancholy feeling or depression of one's spirits that one suffers for no apparent reason. One could say that he was afflicted with the *mubblefubbles* or with the *mulligrubs* or *blue devils*. If the weather remained cloudy day after day, one could complain that the sun god also was in his *mubblefubbles*. The interesting word *stoop-gallant* describes a condition that might well bring about a strong case of the *blue devils*, for it meant something that would humble a proud person. In the early sixteenth century *stoop-gallant* was the name for sweating sickness, a quick and often fatal fever that afflicted both rich and poor and therefore lowered one's pride and made him more understanding of others. A person who suffered from either the *mubblefubbles* or *stoop-gallant* sickness would have responded to the special warmth of an *aimcrier*. Derived from the role of the person who stood near the target and cried "Aim!" to direct an archer and then gave the score, *aimcrier* came to mean the kind of person who would offer approval and encouragement, bolstering another person's spirits and admiring his efforts to succeed.

A magnificent, pithy word, to *fellowfeel* meant more than to sympathize—it meant to feel in earnest how another person feels, to crawl practically under his skin to share his feelings and thereby make him feel better. *Fellowfeeling* people long ago were responsible for originating those marvelous special occasions that were respites from the busy norm, namely *Lifting Monday* and the *love days*. Such people *fellowfelt* with each other by recognizing their mutual aim of ensuring themselves a comfortable *chair day*, the evening of life when one is advanced in age and usually infirm. They thus helped prepare themselves and one another to be able to pass this time of life in peaceful ease and indulgence.

You will soon meet the old words themselves. But one word of caution before you judge their worth: be polite. These old words have waited for centuries to come up from hiding under the dust. They require patience. They look different and sound different. Speed reading would intimidate them into retreating right back under their dust jackets. They are ready for you if you treat them with respect and understanding, if you take the time to examine each on its own merits. The juxtaposition of letters in some is unusual and gives them a humorous look. The compounds are especially colorful, because the union of the two or more words into one, as with *pudding-prick, eyethurl, bellytimber, flesh-spades,* and *downsteepy,* makes us see these separate and combined words in a new light, more meaningful and fresh than before.

This is not a work in which old words are given precise definition; indeed not. Many of these words were gathered from out-of-print sources, and no further clues to corroborate their meanings could be found. Modern lexicographers can defend their interpretations of contemporary words, but since these words are dead no one can be positive about whether there is one definitive way to use them when putting them back into circulation. Many sources have varying definitions, so I have taken the liberty of choosing the ones I found most appealing. Although I use the definitions as the sources gave them, my interpretation of their original shades of meaning must be considered just that, an interpretation, and should not be taken as absolute, for there is only limited evidence to back up how to use these words today. Just as our verb *to know* can have multiple shades of meaning, such as to comprehend by means of information, to gain through inner understanding, to recognize, or to be familiar with, so can we see how difficult or misleading it is to pin down one meaning of an obsolete word as the one and only correct definition. Part of the pleasure of rediscovering these "lost beauties," as Charles Mackay referred to the words he included in his own collection one hundred years ago, comes from letting one's imagination suggest possible nuances of meaning.

I have used the words in forms that I hope will provide pleasure as well as enlightenment. What I call a round is a piece that uses up to eight words and begins and ends with the same word, a device similar to the circular canon in music. (Alastair Reid called this technique a garland in his book *Ounce, Dice, Trice.*) Stories and longer pieces include definitions of the words, some within the text, others next to it, and some elaborated more fully as footnotes. There are as well poems that may seem reminiscent of "Jabberwocky" but these obsolete words *do* have meanings, even though they may sound nonsensical at first. In the short plays, the reader is urged to consult the glossary.

Besides wishing to revive an interest in colorful words that have died, this collection hopes to make people more word conscious in general. Consider the origin of *dandelion,* a flower whose sharply indented leaves resemble *dents de lion,* lion's teeth. Take a moment to repeat simple words like *evening* and *taper,* nouns that stand for what their action verbs literally do. Evening, the time when the light of day comes together with the dark of approaching night, evens out the day with the night, and the taper, a candle, tapers off as it burns. Furthermore, anything that tapers does what a candle does: it slowly melts away. We seldom question as common a word as *breakfast,* which also is a compound word like so many of the Old English words that died. And yet it survived, perhaps because it so aptly defines the meal that breaks the period of not eating for an entire night.

Shakespeare and his contemporaries proved that inventing words can be a challenging and enjoyable pastime, especially if the new words do not merely act as fresh synonyms for existing words but truly fill gaps in our lexicon.

Since compounds like the Old English combinations that are obsolete seem particularly original and evocative upon reexamination, one might hazard a few new compound words to define ideas that lack specific terms today. Let us say that a person has exciting news that he knows it is best not to divulge right away but that he will eventually be at liberty to reveal, such as admission to a college, or pregnancy. A new compound word for the secret that one can hardly contain is *hushbuster.*

The very heart of the matter, the very core of a truth that makes a person say, "That's just what I mean!" could be termed the *pithessence.*

Someone or something that sets the all-time record for making the most money in its own category, be it a movie, an album, an entertainer, or a sports player, would be the *moneypeak* of its field.

A group of nursery school children is, of course, a *totcluster.*

It is embarrassing for a person to realize that

someone has overheard a remark he did not intend the other person to hear. The comment he wishes he could retract is a *blabblurt.*

This book is by no means complete. This very personal collection of lost words, of which there are hundreds more, is an appetizer, an invitation to sample some new words that are actually very old, savor them and, if you like, use them.

A Round of Hum

What is *hum?*
Hum is strong liquor made by combining ale or beer with spirits. Too much *hum* can make one's head *quop.*

What is *quop?*
Quop means to throb. A man's heart may *quop* with longing to hold his loved one's *feat.*

What is *feat?*
A *feat* is a dangling curl of hair. A *woup* with the *feat* of an elephant inside is considered lucky to wear.

What is a *woup?*
A *woup* is a simple metal hoop or ring not set with stones. Large *woups* to anchor one's feet could have been used at the base of a *gofe.*

What is a *gofe?*
A *gofe* is the pillory that was usually erected on the *wong,* where the greatest number of people could stroll by and see it.

What is a *wong?*

A *wong* is the meadowland that people used as their commons, where they would meet or take their cows to graze. Nowadays a public *wong* is covered with *nesh* plantings and lush trees.

What is *nesh?*

Nesh means fresh, delicate, or soft, as vegetables, foliage, or fruit should be. Braiding one's hair with *nesh* flowers makes a beautiful *kell.*

What is a *kell?*

A *kell* is a woman's headdress, be it as close-set as a net or a cap or as fancy as a wig to don for a party. A lady's *kell* is more elaborate if she is going to a ball where *hum* is served.

BELLYTIMBER   *Food.*

GLOP   *To swallow greedily.*

GIVEL   *To heap up.*

REELPOT   *Person who passes the drinking jug around.*

JUBBE   *Large vessel holding liquor.*

VASQUINES   *Petticoats.*

PAGGLE   *To hang loosely or bulge.*

DUMPLE   *To bend or press into a dumpy shape.*

MELPOMENISH   *Tragic, from Melpomene, the Greek muse of tragedy.*

WHOOPUBB   *Obsolete form of* hubbub, excitement, *commotion, from the Gaelic* ubub! *(an interjection of contempt) or from an ancient Irish war cry, "Abu!"*

LENNOW   *Flabby.*

PORKNELL   *Person as fat as a pig.*

EYNDILL   *Jealous.*

FAIRHEADED   *Beautiful.*

YOUNGHEDES   *Youths.*

KEAK   *To cackle, laugh at.*

FELLOWFEEL   *To share the feelings of others, sympathize with.*

NITHE   *Envy, hatred.*

TIPSYCAKES   *Cakes saturated with wine and stuck with almonds, served with custard.*

EARTHAPPLES   *Cucumbers or perhaps potatoes, which in French are* pommes de terre *("apples of the earth").*

In Praise of Bellytimber

Glop the *bellytimber, givel* the plate,
   Let the *reelpot* pass the *jubbe.*
Let *vasquines paggle* and contours *dumple,*
   'Tis not *melpomenish,* nor worth the
     whoopubb.

A *lennow porknell* might be *eyndill*
   Of *fairheaded younghedes* who *keak*
     at his paunch;
But though I *fellowfeel* with his *nithe,*
   I'd rather *tipsycakes* than *earthapples*
     for lunch.

FLAP DRAGON *A game or sport that involved plucking raisins or other objects placed in a bowl of ignited brandy. It was not only a sign of bravado but also a point toward the lover's gallantry for him to toast the health of his lady and drain the cup without burning himself.*

FNAST *From a noun meaning breath and related to the Greek word* pneuma *and the Old English* fnese *'snort or sneeze.'*

Tenderis the Knight

A Medieval Misadventure

Stuff your *flatchet!*   sword
Raise your flagon!
I'm a *mildful* knight   merciful
Who'd risk *flap dragon!*   dangerous sport

sang Tenderis, the Knight, on his way to the castle of his true love, Lay Lady Lay. His horse, *Blonke, fnasted* heavily under the   large horse/snorted weight of his rider and *chamfrain.*   engraved frontlet worn by knight's horse

"Steady on, Blonke. What a good blonke you are! Never *white-livered,* the image of   cowardly *truehead,* like Rosinante. The *scrow* is get-   fidelity/sky ting dark now and my sight's none too keen. When we arrive at the castle I'll get you some *bellytimber* from the *acatery* while you rest   food/storeroom for provisions in your *boose.*   cowstall

As if in response, Blonke chomped on his

HA-HA   *The kind of ditch that one could not see from a distance to avoid. Victims falling into it unaware or witnesses must have given it its fitting name.*

TO KISS THE HARE'S FOOT   *An expression denoting the person who arrives so late that he misses dinner. If he comes too late to partake of the hare, his only option is* to kiss the hare's foot.

KERCHIEF-OF-PLEASANCE   *The embroidered cloth presented by a lady to her knight to wear for her sake. He was bound thereby to attach it to his helmet.*

mastigadour, raised his head, lost his footing, and sank to his knees in a *ha-ha*.

watering bit

ditch

"*'Sheart!* I couldn't see that *ha-ha* in this light. Up, up with you! We must get going!" Tenderis exclaimed as he pulled on Blonke's reins. "Lay Lady Lay is waiting with her *far-net*. We daren't be late or we'll have to *kiss the hare's foot.*"

An oath—"God's heart!"

company of attendants

eat scraps

Blonke got up slowly, trotted a few paces, and stopped, *flerking* one leg and *quetching* until Tenderis dismounted, helped Blonke to sit on his haunches, and examined the horse's leg.

jerking or twitching

uttering moans

"Ah, here's the *breedbate*. A *tingle-nail* caught in your *fairney-cloots*. There! It's out. My lady's *kerchief-of-pleasance* will do for a

mischief maker/tiny tack

horny substance above hoofs

embroidered cloth

ACOPON *A soothing salve or poultice or plaster to relieve pain. In 1661 R. Lovell wrote in a medical journal that "old oil boiled to the temper and thickness of an acopon, helpeth all vices of the nerves and paines."*

WELKIN *From the Saxon words* wealcan *'to roll' and* wolke *'a cloud'. It is also connected to the German word* wolle *'wool', used to describe the woolly quality of clouds. Shakespeare wrote in* A Midsummer Night's Dream,

> The starry *welkin* cover thee anon
> With drooping fog as black as Acheron.

bandage for now till I get an *acopon* for that   poultice
leg and some *ringo* for a treat."   sweet made from candied sea holly root

So Tenderis helped Blonke to his feet and
walked by the horse's side in the direction of
the castle. The two made a sorry pair lumber-
ing in the dark under the weight of their garments and in their discomfort.

"Be not *swerked*, Blonke. I shall sing a   troubled or gloomy
song to my lady. A lay for my Lay Lady Lay!

> The starry *welkin* will not shine   evening sky
> Till you are mine, till you are mine.
> Soon together we'll wine and dine;
> You'll drink to my love; I'll drink
>   to thine.
> A knight am I, sworn only to love,
> Never to fight, nor lay down a glove.
> We'll feather our love-nest, blessed
>   from above,
> I, Tenderis the Knight Owl, my
>   Lady, my Dove!

Tenderis had barely spoken these words
when, neglecting to look where he was walk-
ing, he stepped right into a *drumly flosh*. Try-   muddy/swamp or stagnant pool overgrown with weeds
ing to regain his footing, he blindly reached
for Blonke, who lurched and unwittingly

BARLAFUMBLE *An expression a person would shout when he had fallen in wrestling or play and wanted to have a breather or time out. The word may be a corruption of the French* parlez *or the English parley.*

STOOP-GALLANT *Used here in its primary meaning, an event that would humble a vain person (make a gallant stoop). In the 1500s,* stoop-gallant *specifically referred to a fatal disease that knew no class boundaries.*

ACCLUMSID *From* clumsen, *meaning stiff or numb as though paralyzed and therefore clumsy. A Norwegian counterpart is* clumse, *meaning stiff from the cold.*

CARPET-KNIGHT *A term of contempt that applies to the knight who accomplished more on the carpet of his lady's boudoir than in battle. However, before it came to have this connotation, there was once an order called Knights of the Carpet, who were separate from those sent out to serve in the field.*

TO BREAK ONE'S STEVEN *To fail to keep an appointment. Perhaps the modern phrase "even steven" has to do with this idea of taking set turns or sharing fixed times. Steven itself also meant an outcry or the voice, especially when loud.*

adushed Tenderis's complete fall into the *sloomy* swamp.

    "*Barlafumble!* I give up! This is indeed a *stoop-gallant!* I've soaked my *purfled fewter!* Help me out, Blonke! I'll get the *gwenders* down here. What will lovely Lay Lady Lay think? Will she *snirtle* at such an *acclumsid fopdoodle?* Oh, what a knight! By now, maybe some *nott-headed carpet-knight* is lifting her *flockard* and fondling her *feat!* He

caused

sluggish

call for a truce

setback/decorated/support for lance
tingling from cold

snicker/clumsy

fool or simpleton

closely shorn/rake

veil/dangling curl

could be *spuddling* about the size of his *spit-frog, shabbing* her to break her *steven* with me. I'll *suggill* him with my *snotter-clout —*

bragging/small sword

tricking/appointment

beat/pocket handkerchief

NOSE OF WAX *This term came to be used to describe an accommodating person as easily molded as wax, and was also often used to describe those who changed their faith. Roman Catholics used the term to apply to writers who interpreted the Holy Scriptures in several ways.*

MERRY-GO-SORRY *A gem of a word that juxtaposes the two genuine emotions that one simultaneously feels when experiencing both happiness and sadness.*

PRICK-SONG *Originally a song having all its notes (pricks) written down (pricked), not just memorized. As music became more complex and polyphonic, the term came to mean the musical line or counterpoint that accompanies the main melody.*

CHANTPLEURE *Sing and weep at the same time.*

I'll *frush* him with my *flatchet*—for the sake
of *philotimy!*"

strike or crush/sword
honor

The woeful knight grabbed hold of Blonke's foreleg and pulled himself out of the water. "Ah, well, Blonke, she can't have such a *nose of wax!* 'Tis a *merry-go-sorry* tale to tell. I will compose a pretty *prick-song* about the *samded* knight and his *widdershins* adventure, one that will make her *chantpleure* and give herself to me. On we'll go, damp but undaunted. For this knight is still young. Pressing on, we'll lift our spirits, especially the liquid kind, to the love of Lay Lady Lay!"

fickle personality/joyous and sad
written song
half-dead/unlucky
simultaneously sing and weep

A Smellsmock's Progress

What is a *smellsmock*?
A *smellsmock* is a licentious man, perhaps a former priest, with roving eyes who often has a *paggling* stomach.

What is *paggling*?
Paggling means bulging or hanging down loosely. *Paggling* garments are worn by tired *mumpers*.

What is a *mumper*?
A *mumper* is a beggar who treks from *voil* to *voil*.

What is a *voil*?
A *voil* is a town that benefits from collecting *landcheaps*.

What is a *landcheap*?
A *landcheap* is a fine a person must pay to his lord when he leaves his land. Sometimes officials levy-

ing a *landcheap* require the services of an *oddwoman*.

What is an *oddwoman*?
An *oddwoman* is a female umpire who arbitrates heated arguments. To settle a problem, she may suggest that one party give the other an *assything*.

What is an *assything*?
An *assything* is anything one gives in compensation for an offense he has committed. Apologetic people often *faffle* when offering their assything.

What is *faffle*?
Faffle means to stammer or stumble. One might expect a woman to *faffle* in seeking to escape from a persistent *smellsmock*.

Dretching with a Fearbabe

What is a *fearbabe*?
A *fearbabe* is something a person would use intentionally to frighten a baby. One might expect a *killbuck* to make use of a fearbabe.

What is a *killbuck*?
A *killbuck* is a fierce-looking fellow who deserves a visit to a *kidcote* for his evil deeds.

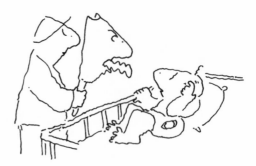

What is a *kidcote?*
A *kidcote* is a special name for a prison. Some kidcotes don't even have an *eyethurl.*

What is an *eyethurl?*
An *eyethurl* is a window such as the one through which the lovely Rapunzel let down her *crinets.*

What are *crinets?*
Crinets are hair. Snarled crinets can *dretch* a child who hates to use a comb and brush.

What is *dretch?*
Dretch means to torment, as one might do with a *fearbabe.* *

* *Note:* For *dretching* the curly *crineted* child with a *fearbabe,* the *killbuck* was sent to a *kidcote* without an *eyethurl.*

SWELCHIE *A whirlpool. Also a local name for a race held in Pentland Firth. In 1688 a J. Wallace described Orkney Island as follows: "On the North side of the isle . . . is a part of the Firth called the Swelchie of Stroma . . . very dangerous."*

Young Tenderis Meets the Eerie Spirit

Before Tenderis was knighted, he endured many tests of strength and dangerous adventures. When he was six years old he had his confrontation with the much-feared Eerie Spirit, who would question him and test his courage. He had heard awful stories from *blob-tales* of how the Spirit would *agruw* boys by *yerding* them with an *elcrooked gaffle* and would then throw them into a *swelchie* if they weren't worthy of being named one of the *ycore*.

  Filled with *ug*, the *younghede* Tenderis groped his way along the *downsteepy* path toward the *cosh* wherein dwelled the feared spirit-person. *Squint-a-pipes* that he was, Tenderis found negotiating his way through the *eileber* and *venenated dway-berries* very

blob-tales — tellers of tall tales/
agruw — horrify
yerding — beating/L-shaped
elcrooked gaffle — heavy metal rod
swelchie — whirlpool

ycore — chosen ones

ug — fear/youth
younghede
downsteepy — precipitous

cosh — hut

Squint-a-pipes — squinting person

eileber — plant used to cure liver disease
venenated dway-berries — poisonous/nightshade berries

TEENFUL *Causing annoyance and vexation, from the word*
teen, *meaning annoyance and irritation. In 1386 Chaucer*
wrote in his Knight's Tale,

> Never was there no word him between
> Of jealousy or any other teen.

In 1594 Shakespeare wrote in Richard III *(Act IV, Scene 1),*
"Each hour's joy wracked with a week of teen."

NABCHEAT *From* nab *'grab, catch, pounce on' plus* cheat,
meaning an article or thing, usually stolen. Perhaps one's
hat was "the thing to grab," a "grab thing."

RECOOPER *Getting something back, in the original sense of*
recovery. *Later,* recovery *came to mean getting back one's*
health, recuperation.

FUCUS *A common term found in seventeenth-century*
poems. Fucus *comes from the identical word in Latin*
meaning rock lichen. Red dye was made from this lichen,
from which rouge was made. Thus "false color" or
"cosmetic paint" became the understood meaning. In 1599
Ben Jonson investigated the ingredients of fucus, *and*
Thomas Dekker suggested using fucus *to get rid of freckles.*

WANG-TOOTH *An alternate form of* wing, *'to the side'.*
Chaucer used this word and wrote of its being situated next
to tushes *'tusks'.*

TITIVIL *From* Titivillus *or* Titinillus, *the name that monks*
gave the devil in their mystery plays. Titivil *passed into*
popular speech undoubtedly because of its repeated use.

teenful in the *nyle*. He tripped over *zuches*
spiss with *maily malshaves* that made him
quetch at their touch. When his *nabcheat*
caught on a *garfangle* hook, he did not stop to
make a *redmod recooper* of it but resolved to
icchen more *hofully* down the path.

     troublesome/fog/
tree stumps/thick/
speckled/caterpillars/
shake or shiver/cap

tall plant with hooked top
hasty/recovery

move/carefully

    Before he could say, "*Xiph* in a *crab-*
skuit," he found himself at the hut. What
would he find inside? A *tutmouthed killbuck*
with *fucus* covering his *wam*, ready to *eye-*
bite him with one glance? A gigantic *verme*, a

small swordfish
open fishing boat

thick-lipped
fierce looking fellow
cosmetic paint/scar/bewitch
legendary Ganges fish
  able to destroy elephants

monstrous *rubb*, or a *trundle-tail*, with one
sharp, deadly *wang-tooth*? As he slowly
opened the door, Tenderis was ready to meet
the devil himself. No *Adaemonist* he. This
was no *fadoodle*. He expected to confront a
wicked *titivil* whose *dweomercraeft* could
turn him into an *irchin*, drive him to *wood-*

Greenland seal
low-bred dog
molar

nonbeliever in the
  devil
nonsense
devil who steals
  names/magic arts

hedgehog/madness

WOODNESS   *From the Old English* wud *or* wood *'out of one's mind'. In 1374 Chaucer wrote in* Troilus, *"They call love a woodness or folly."*

FIREFANGED   *An adjective applied not only to barley or cheese too hastily overheated in the oven so that it dried out but also to burning heretics at the stake.*

PUDDING-PRICK   *The thin skewer to which a bag of pudding was fastened to cook over a fire. Around 1611 it was said of one who squandered away his wealth that he "cut down a mill-post to a pudding-prick."*

FAFFLING   *Simply the echoing sound of a* faff, *a gust of wind. Therefore, to* faffle *meant to blow in sudden gusts.*

TRUCKS   *An English version of an Italian game,* trucco, *which consisted of an upright form called a king placed at one end of a table, at which the player aimed balls.*

ness, or give him the power to *rixle* like an **rule**
athel over the world. **nobleman**

But what is this? Tenderis opened the
door to find no *heanlings* huddling in **base people**
hudder-mudder, preparing to wreak havoc **secrecy**
with their *devilshine.* Instead he *istank* a **demonic powers/smelled**
firefanged smell and perceived his three older **scorched**
brothers stirring a pot, tying the *pudding-* **slender wooden skewer**
prick, and acting like *bluttering aimcriers,* **blustering/applauders**
welcoming him into the hut.

"Well done, you've done it." "You passed
the first test to knighthood!" "Stop *faffling.*" **stammering**
"Grab a *lineseat.*" "We burned the *spitch-* **stool/eel cooked**
cock and cheese, but you're no *fonkin.* Now **with bread crumbs and herbs/little fool**
you're going to be one of us. Care for a game
of *trucks?*" **form of billiards**

Squeck, Vecke, and More

What is *squeck?*
Squeck is a disease that affects fowl. Chickens that suffer from *squeck* are miserable because they feel *yuky.*

What is *yuky?*
Yuky means itchy. A person is *yuky* if he can't get rid of *scrubbado.*

What is *scrubbado?*
Scrubbado is a term for "the itch," a long-forgotten illness cured probably by someone who, upon completing his education, was awarded his *liripoop.*

What is a *liripoop?*
A *liripoop* is the long tail that hung from a graduate's hood—the precursor of the tassel on a mortarboard. Some remarkable *veckes* nowadays return to school and earn new *liripoops.*

What is a *vecke*?
A *vecke* is an old woman. When Queen Elizabeth I
became a *vecke*, she relied on *fardry* to improve
her looks.

What is *fardry*?
Fardry is the act of painting one's face white.
Travelling circus people practice *fardry* on each
other before each performance in a *dingle*.

What is a *dingle*?
A *dingle* is a shady dell, a lowland between hills.
A *dingle* would be a fine place to quarantine birds
afflicted with *squeck*.

Gardyloo! Gardyloo!
Thrip, Shittle, Thrip

What is *shittle?*
Shittle means unstable or inconstant. A person called a *chitty-face* may appear to be *shittle* but turn out to be really rather pleasant.

What is a *chitty-face?*
Chitty-face is a term of contempt for a person who has a thin, pinched face. Practitioners of *flerd* might look *chitty-faced* from all their sneering and selfish scheming.

What is *flerd?*
Flerd is fraud or deceit. A person would be guilty of *flerd* if he promised that using his product would get rid of *murfles.*

What are *murfles?*
Murfles are freckles. *Murfles* have caused many an attractive girl to cry on her *donge* that the fates were unkind to her.

What is a *donge*?
A *donge* is a mattress. *Farture* can make a *donge* soft or hard.

What is *farture*?
Farture is stuffing. Turkey *farture* can be made as quick as a *thrip* with modern mixes that require no baking.

What is a *thrip*?
A *thrip* is a snap of the fingers, as with the thumb and middle finger. A *thrip* hardly suffices to save a passerby if he didn't hear "*Gardyloo!*"

What is a *gardyloo*?
"*Gardyloo!*" is a warning cry that the people of Edinburgh in the 1770s shouted before they threw dirty water from their windows into the street. A good way to punish a *shittle* mate would be to surprise him with a *gardyloo* too late for him to escape.

Ong-tongue *Tattle-tale.*

Brangling *Noisy, wrangling.*

Mung *A crowd of people; also chicken feed. Both definitions deal with mixing together disparate elements.*

Winxing *Braying.*

Felly *Harshly.*

Assything *Compensation for an offense.*

Biting the Ong-tongue

If you hear, in a *brangling mung*,
You're the butt of a *winxing ong-tongue*,
   Lunge for her *felly*,
   Aim for mouth or for belly
Till you've an *assything* wrung.

What Snot Is Not

What is *snot?*
Snot is the burned part of the candle wick. *Snotty* candles would nicely illuminate supper in a *cosh*.

What is a *cosh?*
A *cosh* is a small hut or cottage to retire to after doing your daily *darg*.

What is *darg?*
Darg means a day's work. Part of a farmer's *darg* would be spent preparing *mung*.

What is *mung?*
Mung is a combination of ingredients mixed together to make chicken feed. After a fine meal of *mung* a chicken might *keak* from pleasure.

What is *keak?*
To *keak* means to cackle. Roosters who *keak* too much get *yerded* into submission.

What is *yerd?*
To *yerd* means to beat with a rod. Logs in a fire-
place sometimes need a bit of *yerding* to get a fire
going so that a person can *beek* in peace and quiet.

What is *beek?*
To *beek* is to bask before a fire or in the sun. *Beek-
ing* too long in the sun can make your *pash* red
and painful.

What is a *pash?*
A *pash* is a forehead. A church attendant in charge
of lighting memorial candles spends a great deal of
time with his *pash* over *snots.*

Roaky, Ribble, Drumly, Croodle, and Thring

Scene: *A modern office. The receptionist, Miss Fleak, is seated at desk. The telephone rings and she answers in a nasal, officious voice.*

Receptionist: Roaky, Ribble, Drumly, Croodle, and Thring.

Voice: Hello, is this the firm that deals with family law?

Recep.: Yes, sir. If you're *widdershins* in *poopnoddy*, we can *shab* you of your *mubblefubbles*. What seems to be the problem?

Voice: It's my wife. I think she's a *bedswerver*. And if this continues, it'll upset my *dillings*.

Recep.: Well, perhaps you would like to speak with Mr. Croodle. His specialty is *buck-baskets.*

Voice: I beg your pardon? I'm a bit *pitchkettled.* What did you say?

Recep.: About Mr. Croodle. He delves into the nastiest buck-baskets. That is, he'll clean your dirty linen for you, but never in public. He's a very refined man.

Voice: And how about Mr. Thring?

Recep.: Unlike Mr. Croodle, Mr. Thring loves *faries.* He and his sons—they're his favorite Thrings—love to get their *flesh-spades* into juicy *garboils.*

Voice: No, no. I just want to straighten this thing out quietly without its affecting the children.

Recep.: Well, then, perhaps Mr. Roaky could speak with you. *Storge* is his forte.

Voice: Ah, yes. I dearly love my little ones. I'm so *carked* that they'll be hurt by her *bawdreaming.* My life is completely *kew-kaw.*

Recep.: Oh, I'm so sorry. I forgot that this is *opentide,* and Mr. Roaky is away most of the day. He doesn't come in until *cockshut.*

Voice: When is Drumly in?

Recep.: Now there's a very *straight-fingered* man. Mr. Drumly puts in his *darg* from *sparrow-fart* to *dimpse.* A *kexy* fellow, but reliable and as hard-working as a *blonke.*

Voice: Fine, fine. I'll speak to him, then.

Recep.: As soon as he returns. You see, he lost his two *butter-teeth* in a fallen *scroggling* and can no longer *wheeple.* He's out getting them replaced.

Voice: So who's there for me to talk to, then?

Recep.: Well, Mr. Ribble lost his *thibble,* but if you can stay on the line he'll be back in a minute.

He's a man with a good *inwit*. He'd even give you his *assything*, his *bell-penny*, or some *chap-money* for his services.

Voice: Could you kindly go through your list of *fangers* again?

Recep.: Certainly. There's Roaky, Ribble, Drumly, Croodle, and Thring. And there's . . . Odam.

Voice: What?

Recep.: Not what; who. Odam is the son-in-law of Mr. Roaky. He's not as *roaky* as Mr. Ribble or as ribbled as Mr. Drumly. But then again, Mr. Drumly can be sluggish and doesn't hum along like *Croodle,* who often gets so caught up with *Thrings.* But Odam . . .

Voice: Yes, Odam! Enough of this *reak,* you *fleak!*

Thank you, Erendrake, for Your Yeresyeve

What is an *erendrake?*
An *erendrake* is a messenger whose duties might include posting *pancarts.*

What are *pancarts?*
Pancarts are public notices of the kind that announce that smoking is permitted only in the *crush-room.*

What is a *crush-room?*
A *crush-room* is the room or hall in a theatre in which the audience may gather between acts. Baroque *crush-rooms* were undoubtedly decorated with *knosps* and *ongles.*

What are *knosps* and *ongles?*
A *knosp* is an ornament in the form of a bud or a knob, whereas an *ongle* is a claw. Wood moldings of carved *knosps* and *ongles* might have surrounded a ceiling painted with a scene of Greek

gods and goddesses riding chariots across the *scrow*.

What is the *scrow?*
The *scrow* is the sky, which might inspire an art-ist to sketch with his *scribbet*.

What is a *scribbet?*
Scribbet is charcoal for drawing or even for dash-ing off a quick thank-you note for a *yeresyeve*.

What is a *yeresyeve?*
A *yeresyeve* is a gift given at the new year or upon taking office. Many a *yeresyeve* has been delivered by an *erendrake*.

Poop-noddy *Fool.*

Hardhewer *Stonemason.*

Graffed *Dug.*

Knosp *Architectural ornament shaped like a bud or a knob.*

Cosh *Small cottage.*

Upsy-english *"In the manner of," "English-style."*

Theeked *Covered a roof with protective straw.*

Aimcry *Approve, admire.*

Juvament! *"Help!"*

Hadivist! *An expression of regret for making a mistake, a pang of remorse for having done something in ignorance, as if to say, "If I had only known!" or "I wish I had thought of it before!"*

Eyethurl *Window.*

A Poop-noddy's Mistake

The *hardhewer graffed* for stone for a *knosp*
  For the door to his *cosh, upsy-English* with burl;
He *theeked* it with thatch and stood back to
  aimcry,
  Then shrieked, *"Juvament! Hadivist! No
eyethurl!"*

Penistone Golillas

What is a *golilla?*
A *golilla* is a stiff, starched collar popular in Spain in the seventeenth century. On a Sunday outing, a Spaniard may have donned his *golilla* in search of *barilla.*

What is *barilla?*
Barilla is a water plant found in Spain and Sicily. Used in manufacturing soap, *barilla* helped to keep one's *muckender* clean.

What is a *muckender?*
A *muckender* is a bib or handkerchief easily concealed by a *coverslut.*

What is a *coverslut?*
A *coverslut* is an apron or any garment intended to conceal slovenliness. Yorkshiremen wore *penistone coversluts.*

What is *penistone?*
Penistone is a coarse cloth named after the York-
shire town of Penistone (pronounced "Pennystun")
where it was made. Hand-woven goods made of
penistone cloth may have won prizes at the fair
where *bartholomew-pig* was one of the main
attractions.

What is *bartholomew-pig?*
Bartholomew-pig is the roasted pig displayed and
eaten each year at the Bartholomew Fair in London. A person who ate too much *bartholomew-
pig* paid for his excesses at a local *spittle.*

What is a *spittle?*
A *spittle* is an almshouse or hospital where the
all-purpose panacea was a dose of *slibber-sauce.*

What is *slibber-sauce?*
Slibber-sauce is the slang term for a nauseating
concoction usually given for medicinal purposes.
If *slibber-sauce* was particularly distasteful, a re-
calcitrant patient might spit it out and stain his
golilla.

BELLIBONE *A whimsically anatomical word, an anglicized version of the French expression* belle et bonne *'a fair lass'.*

SANAP *From the Old French* sauvenape *'save the nape' (tablecloth). This particular strip of cloth was placed over the outer edges of the tablecloth to keep it from being soiled.*

TENTERBELLIES *Fat persons. We no longer refer to a* tenter, *a wooden framework on which to stretch cloth so it will not shrink, but do speak of being on tenterhooks, tensely hanging there at the edge of knowing something.* Tenterbellies *therefore means "stretchbellies," people with bellies distended as cloth attached to hooks would be.*

Tenderis's Quest for Romance

Having proved himself on the battlefield, Tenderis's heart *quopped* with the thrill of meeting a different sort of challenge. He vowed to *rixle* over the affections of the latest *bellibone* to catch his fancy, *fairheaded* Pretty Pure Polly Esther. He had *yarkened* a picnic for them to share in a picturesque spot just a *wurp* away from a *brooling* brook, where Tenderis grandly unfolded the *sanap* for their lunch.

    "There's so much to eat!" exclaimed Polly Esther. "We'll gorge ourselves like *tenterbellies! Nesh earthapples* and *fasels* too! Tenderis, help me with this heavy *jubbe* and *zegedines.*"

    "Of course, my lovely Polly. You could *fage* the stars to shine all day. How *mally* I

throbbed or palpitated

rule or have dominion

pretty girl/beautiful

prepared

stone's throw/murmuring

protective cloth

gluttons

fresh/cucumbers
chick-peas and kidney beans
large pitcher

drinking cups

coax/foolishly fond

BACKSTRESS *The female counterpart to* backster, *the forerunner of* baker *and the old spelling of* Baxter, *one of many proper names derived from occupations, such as Cooper and Warden.*

ROBERDAVY *A specific kind of wine consumed in the sixteenth and seventeenth centuries. Since we do not know how it got its name, one can only conjecture that a Robert and a Davy or a Robert Davy thereby achieved immortality.*

ZARF *From the Arabic word for vessel. A* zarf *is a cup made of ornamented metal, as well as a cup-shaped holder for hot coffee.*

BUMBO *A delicious punch made by combining rum, sugar, nutmeg, and water. Its name is borrowed from the word that Italian children use for* drink.

am of you! Taste some of this *bellytimber* I   food
brought. There's no *maw-wallop* here. But,"   badly cooked mess of food
said Tenderis, "I'll just have a bite of the
bread I've bought from the *backstress* and   female baker
wash it down with some *roberdavy*. Fill my   wine
zarf to the brim and I'll drink in your cap-   cup
tivating *wink-a-peeps*."   eyes

    "Be *hoful*, Tenderis. That wine might be   careful
as strong as *hum* from being out in the warm   strong mixture of
sun."   ale or beer and spirits

    "Don't you worry, my Pretty Polly. The
reelpot at the *kidliwink* promised me this   tavern keeper or bartender
wine is light as *aleberry*. Come on. Have   beer shop or *tidliwink*
some. It's mild, not even as sweet as your   ale with sugar, spices and
  bread sops
bumbo. It's so *blashy* it's almost like *Adam's*   rum punch/thin and weak

ADAM'S ALE *A humorous reference to the fact that the only drink that Adam and Eve had available to them was water.*

CONDOG *To concur. An inventive punster must have enjoyed playing with the second syllable by substituting the synonym* dog *for* cur.

POPLOLLY *An affectionate term that comes from the French* poupelet *'little darling' and that came to be applied to a mistress.*

ale. I could drink ten glasses and never feel a   water
thing."

He proffered his cup to Polly Esther.
"Why, I don't *condog* with you at all, Ten-   agree
deris. This tastes as strong as *kill-priest* to   port wine
me. Maybe that *reelpot* is really a *nickpot*   bartender
who gave you *merry-go-down* instead."   fraudulent innkeeper
strong ale

"Now, don't be *carked*, Polly. Just let   fretfully anxious
your mind *dringle* while I drain this one cup   idle lazily
more, and I'll sing you a song." Tenderis,
holding his cup as if in a toast, sang:

Please, please, Pretty Pure Polly,
Please me. Prithee, be my *poplolly;*   little darling or
Pretty please, O Pretty Polly,   a mistress
'Twould be forever, not for folly.

Wouldst I had this Polly Esther,
My love pain, it would not fester;
I'd adore her, never test her,
Be her knight, and not a jester.

No misfortune grand or slight
Can obscure the future bright
For sweet Polly and her knight,
Valiant by day and tender by night.

PISSABED *The term given to the dandelion because of its effect on urine or urination; sources are unclear as to which. A gentleman named T. Lewis Davies wrote, "Wolcot in a note says that the second Lord Chatham was named F.R.S. for presenting some such plant to the Royal Society." Not everyone was in agreement with bestowing membership in the Select Society to Chatham, for a P. Pindar wrote:*

> Through him each trifle-hunter that can bring
> A grub, a weed, a moth, a beetle's wing,
> Shall, to a Fellow's dignity succeed;
> Witness L.C. and his piss-a-bed.

LIRIPOOP *A word with many meanings, its oldest being the long tail that was once part of clerical dress. Later it became part of a graduate's hood and the forerunner of the tassel on a mortarboard. Both meanings could have come from the Latin* cleropeplus *'livery hood'. By the time of Edward III, a* liripoop *came to be a scarf that men donned when dressing extravagantly. As a result of its connection with a graduate, a* liripoop *also came to mean something that had to be learned, like a role or part, as the word is used in this story. A person referred to as one who knows his* liripoop *was considered knowledgeable enough to be entitled to wear the scarf or doctoral hood of the Sorbonne, for example. Still further, Beaumont and Fletcher used the word in* Wit at Several Weapons *to mean a verbal trick, from another term,* lerry-word. *And it has been said that in Devon people use the word to denote a silly person.*

Tenderis reached into the bottom of the picnic basket and began *sparpling* a few *lulibibs* and *kissing-comfits.* "Sweets for the sweet, Polly Esther."

scattering

lollipops/sugar candy or breath sweeteners

He leaned toward Polly for a *lip-clap* but, slightly *turngiddy,* he toppled forward, sprawled on his love, and ended up eye to eye with a *pissabed.*

kiss

dizzy

dandelion

"Tenderis! You *breedbate!* You've knocked me over!" cried Polly Esther, struggling to raise herself up and rearrange her clothing. "You sang such a sweet *liripoop.* Why did you have to spoil it with a *mulwine?*"

mischief-maker

recitation or part

drinking bout

VECKE *Possibly from the Italian* vecchia, *the feminine form of* vecchio *'old'. The* Oxford English Dictionary *qualifies its granting this derivation by explaining, "As direct adoption from Italian would be remarkable in the fourteenth century, it is possible that the word existed in Old French colloquial use."*

"Oh, don't be a silly *vecke!*" replied — old woman
Tenderis. "Do you really think I'm so
feather-headed that I can't hold my cups?" — scatterbrained
He quickly stood up. "I'm not *turngiddy*. — dizzy
Come, let's make a *hand-band.*" — covenant made by joining hands

She let Tenderis take her hand, into
which he thrust a *tisty-tosty* of *bunnikins*. — nosegay
"Will this *lovedrury* of mine convince you to — early spring flowers / love token, keepsake
have a *mentimutation?*" he asked. — change of mind

Polly laughed. "You are filled with surprises, Tenderis. Whenever I'm with you, I
never know what'll *ilimp* next. How can I be — happen
thrunch at someone as *iqueme* as you?" — angry/pleasing, agreeable

Tenderis plucked one *bunnikin* from her — flower
tuzzy-muzzy and, picking the petals from the — nosegay
flower, sang, "She loves me. She loves me
not. She loves me . . . ."

SNAWKY *Nauseating.*

LUBBER-WORT *Food of no nutritive value, "junk food."*

RUTTERKIN *Swaggering boor.*

DINGLE *Shady dell between hills.*

DRETCHING *Tormenting.*

THEOW *Servant.*

DRINGLE *To waste time lazily.*

CRUG *Food. In its original use in the early 1800s at Christ's Hospital School in Hertford, England, it referred to the measly crusts of bread that poor victims there dipped into beer to get some nourishment and taste.*

SLIBBER-SAUCE *Concoctions, especially those used as medicine.*

PINGLE *To eat with little or no appetite.*

Snawky Lubberwort

A *rutterkin* lived in a *dingle,*
Dretching his *theow,* who would *dringle,*
  "Your *crug*'s no great loss,
  Nor your *snawky slibber-sauce.*
Such *lubber-wort* just makes me *pingle!"*

Theeking Shiterows

What is a *shiterow?*
A *shiterow* is a heron who might choose to *theek* her nesting place so no one could steal her eggs.

What is *theek?*
To *theek* means to cover and, in general, protect something. Specifically, it means to cover a roof with straw thatch. In any given *begler-beglic,* people *theeked* their homes in many different styles and patterns.

What is a *begler-beglic?*
A *begler-beglic* is the district over which ruled a *begler-beg,* the governor of a province within the Ottoman Empire. Ranked next to the grand vizier, the *begler-beg* probably had a personal servant to trim his *bugle-beard.*

What is a *bugle-beard?*
A *bugle-beard* is a shaggy beard resembling buffalo hair. A *yetter* should avoid growing a *bugle-beard* or it could get in the way of his work.

What is a *yetter?*
A *yetter* is a metal-caster whose specialized job might be casting the cylindrical molds for *ataballes.*

What are *ataballes?*
Ataballes are kettle-drums, otherwise known as "smurd" in *back-slang.*

What is *back-slang?*
Back-slang is the technique of saying words backwards. One can be showy and toss off a polysyllabic word like "noitacirbulibom" or be modest and settle for two syllables with "gnil-reps" which is *back-slang* for *sperling.*

What is a *sperling?*
A *sperling* is a small, common European smelt as well as a young American herring. While hoping to catch a *sperling*, a quiet fisherman may be lucky enough to spot a *shiterow.*

A Walk through the *Wong*

Miss Fleak, formerly the receptionist of Roaky, Ribble, Drumly, Croodle and Thring, has a new position as one of the operators on the answering service for the police headquarters.

Caller: Hello! Police? My *trantles* have been stolen!

Fleak: I am sorry, sir, but all the officers are out celebrating at their *bean-feast.* This is the answering service. May I help you?

Caller: No! I don't want to talk to some *afterling!* I want the chief of police!

Fleak: I told you, sir, he's out *glopping* his *bellytimber.* When he returns, I'll give him your message.

Caller: Yes, yes, all right. Please write everything down. I don't want anyone to *misgloze* what happened to me.

Fleak: Certainly. I'll take down every word.

Caller: You see, I was on my way out of town, carrying my suitcase filled with all of my most valuable possessions. Some people might call them *trantles,* but to me they mean a lot.

Fleak: Oh, I know what you mean, sir. My handbag is like a *bulse* to me.

Caller: Well, I took a short-cut through the Boston *Wong.*

Fleak: Through Boston Wong? Oh, it's so lovely there! The *nesh* flowers in spring, the *shiterows* in the river . . .

Caller: Miss! Are you listening? I'm telling you a *melpomenish* story and you're talking *fadoodle!*

Fleak: Sorry, sir. You were saying about the Wong?"

Caller: The trees were *purfled* with snow and I stopped for a minute and put down my suitcase, mind you, for just one instant, to watch a few children *hurley-hacket* before *cockshut.*

Fleak: Sorry to interrupt, sir, but I seem to have dropped my *dentiscalp* and I'm . . . looking . . . around . . . Ah! Here it is. Go on, sir.

Caller: My suitcase! It was suddenly gone!

Fleak: Gone? Where did you lose it?

Caller: How can you ask me that? I didn't lose it—someone stole it! I just hope you're *pricking* this down! You don't seem to understand! Someone sneaked up on me and . . .

Fleak: Are you sure? You know, you can't just call everyone you meet a *wind-sucker.*

Caller: Some *yisser* made off with my luggage. That's why I'm calling the police! If there were more *streetmen* around, this never would have happened!

Fleak: Quite right, sir, right you are. Why, one day I opened my *bubble-bow* to give a *mumper* some *chinkers* just to get him to stop *thigging,* and he upped and grabbed the whole bubble-bow, and ran off!

Caller: And those cops right now are out at their bean-feast while *magsmen* are practicing *figging-law* all over town!

Fleak: Now really, sir, some charity, if you please! All of our officers are decent men, no *gattoothed rutterkins,* and the chief won't allow any *acerse-*

comics on his force, no sir! And none of them has ever been caught collecting *dead pay*, either.

Caller: Okay, okay. I looked around me for the culprit. And sure enough, in the distance I saw the thief or his *cloyer tittuping* through the snow with my suitcase tucked under his *okselle*.

Fleak: Right or left?

Caller: Right or left what?

Fleak: Okselle, sir.

Caller: What difference does that make?

Fleak: I just want to get down all the facts, sir. Did you run after him?

Caller: Of course! But he ducked into an alley. It was already *dimpse* and the sun had gone down.

And I lost sight of him. I found only a small *yepsen* of change in my pocket, so I called you.

Fleak: Good thinking. Can you give me a description of the thief?

Caller: I never saw him close enough. He was fast. He must have done quite a bit of *snapsauce* when he was very young and gone on from there. I hope for his sake he's *flag-fallen* and maybe getting some things he needs from my loss and isn't just a prankster who plays *bubble-the-justice* for a lark.

Fleak: Now what was inside your suitcase?

Caller: Everything I've ever *iswonken* for! All my clothes. But that's nothing compared to having lost my little treasures, my one-and-only *liripoop!*

Fleak: Your liripoop! That is a great loss.

Caller: And my silver *orlings!* Irreplaceable! I hope my *golilla* gives him *merry-galls!*

Fleak: Silver orlings . . . did you say *golilla?*

Caller: Yes, handmade from only the finest cloth. Fie on his needs! *Whisterpoops* are too good for the scoundrel!

Fleak: Whisterpoops . . .

Caller: No, no! That doesn't go on the list! Am I *umbecast* by incompetents? Why are there no magistrates when you need them? Why must I get an operator who's a *fleak!*

Fleak: Why, yes! I'm Miss Fleak. How clever of you to know my name!

Caller: Oh! It's my luck to be plugged in to you!

Fleak: Why, thank you! And please go on with your story. It's so exciting! Can you hear me? Is there something wrong with our connection? Hello . . . Hello! . . . Oh, I seem to have lost him . . . such a nice man. He remembered me and I never even got his name or number!

Presenting the Prickmedainty

What is a *prickmedainty?*
A *prickmedainty* is a dandy, a person who is very finicky about his or her style of dress. Female *prickmedainties* apply *calliblephary* as the final pièce de résistance.

78

What is *calliblephary?*
Calliblephary is coloring for the eyelids. Only *dweomercraeft* can transform an ugly hag, who can't expect *calliblephary* to make her irresistible.

What is *dweomercraeft?*
Dweomercraeft is the art of magic or juggling. A star performer of *dweomercraeft* whose fame has gone to his head may lose all his appeal by exhibiting and expecting gross *pumpkinification* in public.

What is *pumpkinification?*
Pumpkinification is exaggerated praise or pompous behavior. Like any other human quality, *pumpkinification* can be *agathokakological* to one's self-image.

What is *agathokakological?*
Agathokakological means comprised of good and evil. If one's *agathokakological* balance is weighted to one side, one might resort to leveling *whistersnefets* at an adversary during an argument.

What are *whistersnefets?*
A *whistersnefet* is a blow or buffet, like a slap on the ear. Whistersnefets are a source of *adlubescence* for masochists.

What is *adlubescence?*
Adlubescence means pleasure or delight. If consummate *adlubescence* is your only quest you

might spurn the little pleasures of life and fall
victim to *floccinaucinihilipilification.*

What is *floccinaucinihilipilification?*
Floccinaucinihilipilification is the habit of belittling achievements of others. A jealous cynic may
indulge in *floccinaucinihilipilification,* belittling
the painstaking efforts another has made in maintaining his reputation as a *prickmedainty.*

Name Calling

The popular sport of name calling has probably existed since the beginning of time. When one looks over the wealth of choice derogatory terms that are now defunct, one decries this loss. The obsolete words seem to be aimed at people in four categories: base, contemptible persons and bullying braggarts; fat, greedy people; fools; women.

Base, contemptible persons and bullying braggarts

Consider the mileage to be gained from calling an adversary not just contemptible but a *mumper*, *lickspittle*, or *lickspigot*. These names are akin in that the *mumper* begged and sponged off others, whereas the *lickspittle* or *lickspigot* was an even more revolting parasite who hung on, even to lick the last drop from a spigot.

Hoodpick and *giveler* are related in that the *hoodpick*, a miser or skinflint, was one degree above the *giveler*, who probably deserved this term of contempt for his avaricious habit of hoarding things for himself.

A *heanling* was a low, base person, the kind you wouldn't give a second thought to kicking aside, whereas a *whifling* was so onomatopoetically insignificant as to be worthy of being called practically nothing at all.

A *killbuck* resembled a *killcow* in one respect only: both looked fierce enough to terrorize—to cow—another person. But the term *killcow* went further. It applied also to a murder-

ous type of fellow, a real butcher, of the notorious kind that inspired this ballad from the 1600s advising against becoming a meat dealer:

> Of all occupations that nowadays are used
> I would not be a butcher, for that's to be
>   refused;
> For whatever is gotten, or whatever is gained,
> He shall be called killcow, and so shall be
>   named.

Killcow was also the term for a person who thought he was a somebody, a braggart who earned his sobriquet by intimidating helpless women who, like cows, were unwarlike, placid creatures and therefore easy to bully. This type of killcow was comparable to the swaggering swashbuckler known as a *rutterkin*, for both were full of their own inflated self-images and were worthy of such windy-sounding nicknames as *huff-muff*, *huff-snuff*, *huff-nose*, and *hufty-tufty*.

Be he *killcow*, *killbuck*, or *rutterkin*, the *waghalter* went beyond swashbuckling, threatening, and terrorizing; he deserved to *wag* 'swing' on the *halter* 'gallows', for having committed an evil offense.

Not merely a licentious man, the term smellsmock referred as early as 1550 to an errant clergyman. In 1634 a gentleman named Thomas Heywood wrote in his book *Maidenhead, Well Lost*, "I think you'll prove little better than a *smellsmock*, that can find out a pretty wench in such a corner." One can therefore deduce a double interpretation of the word. The term *smellsmock* would apply not only to a man of God whose extra-curricular activities gave him a smelly smock but also to a lecherous womanizer who knew how to "smell a smock," that is, to recognize an easy conquest.

Fat, greedy people

Gluttons were guilty of *aletude*, fatness of the body. A person we might call gross today used to be called such terms as *porknell, gundygut, greedigut,* or *tenterbelly.*

The *porknell* was, as the term implies, as fat as a pig. *Gundygut* and *greedigut* carried more derogatory overtones and characterized the person who ate voraciously, offensively, and with no manners at all. The *tenterbelly* was one who had his stomach literally stretched to its farthest capacity, as cloth was formerly stretched on hooks.

Fools

Fools have always been around for others' pleasure, but they are no longer designated by such lively names as *fopdoodle,* a word for an ordinary simpleton or fool. *Fonkin* was a diminutive, almost affectionate-sounding word for a little fool who possessed more charm perhaps than the silly *fopdoodle*.

A *hoddypeak* was a stupid blockhead, as were the *hoddy-noddy* and the *hoddypoll*.

Interestingly enough, the term *poop-noddy* meant not only a fool but also the game of love, in which most people might become giddy or silly.

The simple fool who proved himself to be "soft in the head" was nicknamed *velvet head* and was thereby compared to a young deer whose horns were still covered with soft velvet.

And, finally, the fool who was called a *mobard* was the kind of clown who was more boorish than amusing.

Women

Women seemed especially vulnerable as targets and were most definitely not exempt from insult. Probably some early terms for certain kinds of women are extinct because standards of taste deemed them unprintable. A few that remain are *fleak, tirliry-puffkin,* and *fizgig.*

The two dialogues in this book feature Miss Fleak, a not-too-bright insignificant creature who exemplifies her name. She might also have been called a *tirliry-puffkin,* the term for a lightheaded, flighty woman. More dizzy and frivolous was the *fizgig,* a woman who, without her *gig,* or senses about her, flew off in different directions, like the fizzing paper firework of the same name.

A woman was termed *fliperous* if she was both a minx and a proud gossip. Proud in demeanor also, the *tittup* paraded about by walking with an up-and-down movement like the prancing of a horse, the sound of whose feet while cantering was "tittup, tittup." But who is to say whether or not the pun implicit in this onomatopoetic term for a forward hussy is truly unintentional?

Wallydraigle, drassock, and *daggle-tail* or *draggle-tail* are three names that apply to a slovenly woman. Both the *wallydraigle* and the *drassock* were drab, unkempt, untidy, and worthless women, whereas the *daggle-tail* or *draggle-tail* wore garments that became sloppy and dirty by their being trailed over wet ground.

It is only a short step from a woman's wearing filthy skirts to her being called a slut, as the *daggle-tail* and others came to be called. The slovenly *drossell,* whose epithet had as many variations *(drotchell, dratchell, drazell)* as a musical piece, was exploited as crassly as the *taw-bess,* another name for a slattern. The male who called a woman the abusive term *whipperginnie* revealed himself to be an outright user of women, for this term, like *whip-her-jenny,* conveyed his disrespect for her and his disregard for her right to retain her virginity. Curiously, the word eventually became the name of a card game and the phrase "land of whipperginnie" a nickname for purgatory.

Older women as well were accorded special words showing contempt. The *bronstrops* or *bawdstrot* was not only a prostitute but also a procuress. To call a woman a *walking mort* was the ultimate insult. Like "moving death," she was a despicable sight—a grown-up, unmarried whore who often pretended to be a widow, acting out a transparent charade.

Not all names were derogatory of course. A man who had a favorite mistress might have playfully referred to her as his *poplolly,* from the French *poupelet* 'darling' and have paid her a compliment by calling her a *bellibone.* A corruption of the French adjectival phrase *belle et bonne* 'fair and good', the term meant a fair maid or a bonny (perhaps from *bonne* again) lass. Let's not forget the *boonfellow,* a warm companion, or those people who expressed their *merry-go-sorry* feelings, mixed feelings of joy and sorrow. *Fellow-feelers* did exist. But the derisive terms seem somehow more prevalent—and a lot more fun.

Glossary

Aids to pronunciation are given where necessary and when available.

ACATERY   Around the year 1400, provisions purchased for a king as well as the name of the room in which they are stored. *Acatery* derived from French *acheter* 'to buy'. The officers in charge of an *acatery* were a sergeant, two joint clerks, and yeomen who supervised meat, grain, delicacies, and salt.

ACCLUMSID   Numbed, paralyzed, clumsy. From the Old English *clumsen* 'to be stiff, numb'.

ACERSECOMIC   One whose hair was never cut. From the Greek.

ACOPON   A soothing salve, poultice, or plaster to relieve pain.

ADAEMONIST   A person who denies belief in the devil.

ADAM'S ALE   A humorous term for water, the only drink for Adam and Eve.

ADLUBESCENCE (accent on *bes*)   Pleasure, delight.

ADUSH (accent on *ush*)   To cause to fall heavily, to precipitate.

AFTERLING   An inferior.

AGATHOKAKOLOGICAL (accent on *log*)   With a mingling of good and evil.

AGRUM   A swelling of the cheeks or mouth.

AGRUW (accent on *gruw*)   To horrify, to cause shuddering.

AIMCRIER   An applauder, encourager, the person who cried "Aim!" to encourage an archer; the one who stood near the target to report the results of each round.

ALEBERRY   Ale boiled with spices, sugar, and sops of bread.

ALETUDE   Obesity, bodily fatness.

ASSYTHING   (accent on *syth*, pronounced *sithe*)   Something given as compensation for an offense; reparations.

ATABALLES   Kettle-drums.

ATHEL (accent on *a*)   A nobleman.

BACK-SLANG   The technique of pronouncing words backwards.

BACKSTRESS   A female baker.

BARILLA (accent on *rill*)   A marine plant from Spain and Sicily used in manufacturing soap.

BARLAFUMBLE   A call for a truce by a person who has fallen in play or wrestling; a request for time out.

BARTHOLOMEW-PIG   Roasted pig displayed and eaten at

the annual Bartholomew Fair on Saint Bartholomew's Day, August 24, from 1133 to 1855, in London. Shakespeare used it as a derisive term for Falstaff.

BAWDREAMING   Bawdy misbehavior.

BAWDSTROT.   See *bronstrops.*

BEAN-FEAST   An annual dinner given by employers for their workers in the late 1800s in England. Its name comes from the appearance of beans at the table or the serving of a bean goose whose bill resembled a horse-bean. It is possible also that the name comes from the Middle English word *bene* 'prayer, solicitation', since it was the custom to solicit or take up collections for the common good at that occasion.

BEDSWERVER   A person unfaithful to the marriage bed. Synonym: *spousebreak.*

BEEK   To bask in the sun or before a fire.

BEGLER-BEGLIC   A district over which ruled a *begler-beg,* the governor of a province in the Ottoman Empire, who ranked next to the grand vizier.

BELLIBONE   A lovely maiden, a pretty lass. An anglicization of the French *belle et bonne* 'fair and good'.

BELL-PENNY   Money one saves for his own funeral.

BELLYTIMBER   Food, provisions.

BLASHY   Thin or weak, as applied to tea or beer.

BLOB-TALE   A tattle-tale or gossip. Synonym: *ong-tongue.*

BLONKE   A large, powerful horse.

BLORE   To cry out or bleat and bray like an animal.

BLUTTER   To blurt out.

BOONFELLOW   A warm companion.

BOOSE   A cow stall.

BRANGLE   Verb: to squabble or brawl; noun: a muddle or state of confusion.

BREEDBATE   A person or something that creates strife; a mischief maker.

BRONSTROPS   A prostitute.

BROOL   A low, deep humming, a murmur.

BUBBLE-BOW   A lady's tweezer box or pocketbook. Perhaps originally a misspelling of *bauble-buoy,* a container for baubles.

BUBBLE-THE-JUSTICE   "Cheat the magistrate"—a nineteenth-century game of nine holes. From *bubble* 'dupe'.

BUCK-BASKET   A large basket to carry dirty linen. From *buck* 'bleach' and Celtic *buac,* cow dung mixed with other materials to make lye for bleaching linen.

BUGLE-BEARD   A shaggy beard like buffalo hair.

BULSE   A package of diamonds or gold dust. The word comes from the medieval Latin *bursa* 'purse'.

BUMBO   Italian, a child's word for *drink;* a punch made of rum, sugar, water, and nutmeg.

BUTTER-TEETH   The two upper middle incisors.

CALLIBLEPHARY (accent on *bleph*)   A coloring for eyelids. From the Greek words *kallos* 'beauty' and *belepharon* 'eyelid'.

CARKED   Fretfully anxious.

CARPET-KNIGHT   A derogatory term for a knight who achieved more on the carpet of a lady's boudoir than in battle; the Knights of the Carpet, an order of knights so called to distinguish them from those who served in the field.

CHAIR DAY   The evening of life, that time when a person is old and usually infirm but passes his time in ease and comfort.

CHAMFRAIN   The frontlet of an armed horse for a feudal knight, often engraved with designs.

CHANTPLEURE   To sing and weep at the same time.

CHAP-MONEY   Small sums returned to the buyer when he pays for a purchase—a discount. From Old English *ceap* 'barter, deal'. A *chapman* was one who made deals.

CHINKERS   Money, coins.

CHITTY-FACE   A person with a thin, pinched face; a term of contempt.

CLOYER   A pickpocket's accomplice or the one who intrudes into a bunch of thieves to claim a share.

COCKSHUT   Twilight; the time poultry are shut up for the night.

CONDOG   To agree; a pun on *concur*.

CORSNED   The ordeal by bread, a medieval test to determine guilt. The accused was ordered to swallow an ounce of bread consecrated by a priest with an exorcism. If he went into convulsions he was pronounced guilty, but if he had no reaction he was proclaimed innocent. From the Old English *cor* 'trial' and *snaed* 'piece'.

COSH   A small cottage, hut.

COVERSLUT   An apron; an architectural decoration to cover ugliness or deformity.

CRAB-SKUIT   A small, open fishing boat with sails.

CRINET   A hair.

CROODLE   To creep close; a faint humming, the low music of birds.

CRUG   Food (slang), from crusts of bread at Christ's Hospital School in Hertford, England, dipped in beer to add taste.

CRUNKLE   To cry like a crane.

CRUSH-ROOM   A room or hall in a theatre in which the audience could stroll between acts.

CUCKING-STOOL   A chair for punishment in which the offender was fastened, to be jeered at publicly or dunked in a lake or river.

DAGGLE-TAIL   A woman whose garments are dirtied by being trailed over wet ground, so by extension an untidy woman, a slut or slattern.

DARG   A day's work.

DEAD PAY   Pay continued to a dead soldier that is taken by dishonest officers for themselves.

DENTISCALP   A toothpick. From the Latin *dens* 'tooth' and *scalpere* 'to scratch'.

DEVILSHINE   Demonic power or skill.

DILLING   A child born when the parents are old; possibly a corruption of *darling; dilling-pig,* the weakling in a litter.

DIMPSE   The dimming of daylight, twilight. See also *cockshut.*

DINGLE   A shaded dell, a hollow between hills. Also *dimble, dumble.*

DONGE   A mattress.

DOWNSTEEPY   Steeply descending, precipitous.

DRAGGLE-TAIL   See *daggle-tail.*

DRASSOCK   A drab, untidy woman.

DRETCH   To torment.

DRINGLE   To waste time in a lazy manner. Also *drubble, drumble.*

DROSSELL   A slut, hussy. Also *drazell.*

DRUMLY   Cloudy, sluggish. From Old English *droum* 'mud'.

DUMPLE   To bend or compress into a dumpy shape.

DWAY-BERRY   The berry of the deadly nightshade, resembling black cherries.

DWEOMERCRAEFT (accent on o)   Juggling, the magic arts.

EARTHAPPLE   A cucumber or potato. Perhaps from the French *pomme de terre* 'potato', literally "apple of the earth."

EAUBRUCHE   Adultery.

EILEBER   A plant used as a remedy for liver disease and lumbago.

ELCROOKED   L-shaped.

ELDNYNG   Jealousy, suspicion.

ERENDRAKE   A messenger.

EYEBITE   To bewitch with the eye.

EYETHURL   A window.

EYNDILL   Jealous.

FADOODLE   Nonsense, something foolish.

FAFFLE   To blow in sudden gusts; to stammer or fumble. From the echoing sound of a *faff* 'gust of wind'.

FAGE   To coax, flatter, beguile.

FAIRHEAD   Beauty.

FAIRNEY-CLOOTS   Small horny substances above the hoofs of horses, sheep, and goats.

FANGER   A guardian, one who protects, as do fanged animals.

FARDRY   The act of painting the face white.

FARNET   A company of attendants.

FARTURE   Stuffing.

FARY   A state of consternation, tumult.

FASELS   Chick-peas, kidney beans.

FEARBABE   A thing designed to scare a baby.

FEAT   A dangling curl of hair.

FEATHER-HEAD   A silly, lightheaded person.

FELLOWFEEL   To share another's feelings, to sympathize with.

FELLY   Harshly, destructively.

FEWTER   A support for a lance or spear attached to a knight's saddle.

FIGGING-LAW   The practice of cutting purses and picking pockets.

FIREFANGED   Scorched; overheated and producing a singed taste or smell.

FIVE EGGS ("to come in with one's five eggs")   A sixteenth-century expression meaning to interrupt with a trivial story and to make an offer not worthwhile to the other party. From the cheap price of eggs; "to have eggs on the spit," an expression meaning very busy.

FIZGIG   A frivolous person, especially a woman. Fireworks in the form of a serpent. Paper is rolled around a roller the width of a little finger and one end of the roller is filled with fireworks material.

FLAG-FALLEN   Unemployed. From the sixteenth- and seventeenth-century custom of lowering a playhouse flag when no performance was held and the actors were out of work.

FLAP DRAGON   The sport of catching raisins in bowls of flaming brandy or drinking the brandy without getting burned as a tribute to one's mistress.

FLATCHET   A sword.

FLEAK   A pejorative term for a woman; an insignificant person.

FLERD   Deceit, fraud.

FLERK   To jerk or twitch.

FLESH-SPADES   Fingernails.

FLIPEROUS   A proud gossip, a prattler.

FLOCCINAUCINIHILIPILIFICATION (accented on *ca*)   The habit of estimating things as worthless and belittling others' achievements. A term coined by linking four words in an Eton Latin grammar book *flocci-nauci-nihili-pili-fication*. Sir Walter Scott wrote of the *floccinaucinihilipilification* of money.

FLOCKARD   A veil floating from a headdress.

FLOSH   A swamp or stagnant pool overgrown with weeds.

FNAST   To pant, snort.

FONKIN   A little fool.

FOPDOODLE   A simpleton.

FRUSH   To crush, strike, break. From the Latin *frustum* 'fragment'.

FUCUS   Rouge made from rock lichen, which produced a red dye. This false color became a cosmetic cover-up.

GANG-TEETH   Projecting teeth.

GARBOIL   Turmoil, commotion, from the Old French word *garbouille*, of the same meaning. The earlier Celtic word *garblough* meant a heavy or rough blow.

GARDYLOO   In old Edinburgh, a warning cry before throwing dirty water from windows into the street in the 1770s. From the French *gare l'eau* 'beware of the water'.

GARFANGLE HOOK   A plant reaching a height of eight feet with a hook on the top.

GATTOOTHED   Having teeth set wide apart. From the Old English *gat* 'gap'.

GIVEL   To heap up. *Giveler* was a term of contempt for a greedy person.

GLEED   Squint-eyed, one-eyed; also crooked.

GLOP   To swallow greedily; to stare at in wonder or alarm.

GOFE   The pillory.

GOLILLA   A stiff, starched collar worn in Spain in the seventeenth century. From the Latin *gula* 'throat'. Also related to gullible; capable of swallowing anything.

GRAFF   To dig.

GUNDYGUT   A glutton. Also *greedigut*.

GWENDERS   A disagreeable tingling from the cold.

HADIVIST   An expression meaning had I known, to express regret at making a mistake or letting an opportunity go by.

HA-HA   A sunken trench or ditch not visible until one steps into it. From the Anglo Saxon *hoeh* meaning hole.

HAND-BAND   A covenant made by joining hands.

HARDHEWER   A stonemason.

HEANLING   A humble or base person.

HODDYPEAK   A simpleton, blockhead.

HOFUL   Careful.

HOODPICK   A miser or skinflint.

HUDDER-MUDDER   Secrecy, privacy.

HUFTY-TUFTY   A braggart or conceited boor. Also *huff-muff, huff-snuff, huff-nose.*

HUM   A strong liquor, a mixture of ale or beer and spirits.

HURLEY-HACKET   The sport of tobogganing.

ICCHEN   To move, stir.

ILIMP   To happen, befall.

INWIT   Conscience, knowledge from within, as opposed to *outwit*, acquired knowledge.

IQUEME   Pleasing, agreeable.

IRCHIN   A hedgehog; a dish with almonds on top bearing a similarity to a hedgehog.

ISTINK   Transitive verb: to smell.

ISWONK   Toil.

JUBBE   A large vessel for liquor.

JUVAMENT   Aid!, help!

KEAK   To cackle.

KELL   A woman's headdress, cap.

KERCHIEF-OF-PLEASANCE   An embroidered cloth presented by a lady to her knight to wear for her sake. He was bound by the code of honor to put it on his helmet.

KEW-KAW   Upside-down.

KEXY   Dry, juiceless.

KIDCOTE   A prison; from the name of a specific prison in York, England.

KIDLIWINK   A beer shop, a *tidliwink.*

KILLBUCK   A fierce-looking fellow.

KILLCOW   A braggart, swashbuckler, or bully; a murderous fellow, a butcher.

KILL-PRIEST   Port wine.

KISS THE HARE'S FOOT   To be so late as to miss dinner and be able only to kiss the animal's foot; i.e., to eat left-over scraps.

KISSING-COMFITS   Sweets to make the breath pleasant.

KNOSP   An architectural ornament in the form of a bud or knob.

LANDCHEAP   A fine paid to the lord of a manor when leaving his land.

LENNOW   Flabby, limp.

LICKSPIGOT   One who fawns or behaves in a servile manner. Also *lickspittle, lickdish.*

LIFTING MONDAY   Easter Monday in the 1800s, when it was the custom in Lancashire for men to lift up and kiss each woman they met. On Easter Tuesday women could do likewise for the men. The custom was stopped because of the disturbances it caused.

LINESEAT   A stool to use while spinning.

LIP-CLAP   Kissing.

LIRIPOOP   A tail that hung from a graduate's hood, the precursor of the modern tassel on a mortarboard; a decorative scarf; a storehouse of knowledge; a role or part, something to be learned; a trick, or a silly person.

LOVECUP   A local market duty, tax.

LOVE DAYS   Certain days appointed to settle differences between parties by amicable arbitration.

LOVEDRURY   A keepsake, love token.

LUBBER-WORT   Food or drink that makes one idle and stupid. Food of no nutritional value, "junk food."

LULIBUB   Early form of *lollipop.*

MAGSMAN   A swindler.

MAILY   Speckled.

MALLY   Foolishly fond.

MALSHAVE   Caterpillar.

MASTIGADOUR   A watering bit for a horse.

MAW-WALLOP   A badly cooked mess of food.

MELPOMENISH (accent on *pom*)   Tragic. From Melpomene, the Greek muse of tragedy.

MENTIMUTATION   A change of mind.

MERRY-GALL   A sore produced by chafing.

MERRY-GO-DOWN   Strong ale.

MERRY-GO-SORRY   A tale that evokes mixed feelings of joy and sorrow.

MILDFUL   Merciful.

MISGLOZE   To misinterpret.

MOBARD   Clown, boor. A term of contempt.

MUBBLEFUBBLES   A depression of the spirits for no reason, melancholy. Also *blue devils, mulligrubs.*

MUCKENDER   A bib or handkerchief.

MULWINE   A drinking bout.

MUMPER   A beggar, one who sponges off others.

MUMPOKER   A word used to frighten naughty children.

MUNG   Food for chickens; a crowd of people.

MURFLES   Freckles, pimples.

NABCHEAT   A hat, cap.

NESH   Fresh, delicate, soft; applied to fruit, vegetables, and foliage.

NICKPOT   A fraudulent innkeeper.

NITHE   Envy, hatred.

NOSE OF WAX   A fickle personality, anything accommodating; also, applied to one's flexibility of faith as a means of protecting oneself; and also to describe Catholic writers who variously interpreted the Holy Scriptures.

NOTT-HEADED, NOTT-PATED   Having hair closely cut, from the Saxon *hnot.*

NYLE   Fog, mist.

ODAM (accent on *o*)   A son-in-law.

ODDWOMAN   A female umpire or arbitrator.

OKSELLE   Armpit.

ONGLE   Claw.

ONG-TONGUE   See *blob-tale.*

OPEN-TIDE   Early spring, the time when buds open.

ORLINGS   Teeth of a comb.

ORMUZINE   A fabric brought from Ormuz, near the entrance to the Persian Gulf, in the 1600s.

OUTWIT   Knowledge, information, learning one gains from outside oneself.

PAGGLE   To bulge, hang loosely.

PANCART   A placard with public notices.

PASH   The forehead. From the Gaelic *bash* or *pash,* the root word for *abash,* browbeat, intimidate.

PENISTONE (pronounced *pennistun*)   Coarse woollen cloth woven in the town of Penistone, England.

PHILOTIMY   Love of honor.

PINGLE   To eat with very little appetite.

PISSABED   A name given to the dandelion for its diuretic effects.

PITCHKETTLED   Puzzled, from the Scotch word *kittled.*

POOP-NODDY   A fool or simpleton; the game of love.

POPLOLLY   A little darling (from the French *poupelet*); a female favorite, special loved one, or mistress.

PORKNELL   One as fat as a pig.

PRICKMEDAINTY   A dandy, a person of either sex who is finicky about his or her style of dress. From one meaning of *prick,* which is to pin somebody up, thus to dress up elaborately. John Skelton wrote a ridiculing verse, "The Tunnying of Elynour Rummyng," in 1829.

PRICK-SONG   A song in which the notes were written (*pricked*) down, as opposed to a plain-song, which was not recorded; also harmony.

PUDDING-PRICK   A slender wooden skewer with which the ends of gut containing pudding were fastened.

PUMPKINIFICATION   Pompous behavior or exaggerated praise. From incorrect Greek translation of a word meaning divinity in a text by Seneca.

PURFLE   To decorate, adorn.

QUETCH   To moan and twitch in pain, shake.

QUOP   To throb, palpitate.

REAKS   Pranks, practical jokes.

RECOOPER   Recovery.

REDMOD   Hasty, rash.

REELPOT   One who makes a drinking pot go around.

RIBBLE   A wrinkle, furrow.

RIDING THE STANG   A form of public ridicule formerly practiced in parts of England, Scotland, and Wales to punish a husband for beating or betraying his wife. A parade was formed in which the guilty party was carried through the streets and denounced by the populace or exposed to humiliation through derisive verse. See *skimmington*.

RINGO   A treat; a sweet made from the candied root of the sea holly, supposed to be an aphrodisiac.

RIXLE   To rule, have dominion.

Roaky   Hazy, nebulous, not clear, from the French word *rauque*, pertaining to the voice, meaning hoarse or thick.

Roberdavy   A kind of wine in the sixteenth and seventeenth centuries.

Rooped   Hoarse, as with bronchitis or a throat cold.

Rubb   A seal or sea dog from Greenland.

Rumfordize   To improve a smoky chimney according to a system invented by Sir Benjamin Thompson, the Count von Rumford, in the early 1800s.

Rutterkin   A swaggering gallant or bully.

Samded   Half-dead. From the Old English *sam* and the Latin *semi*.

Sanap   A strip of cloth placed over the outer part of tablecloth to keep it from being soiled.

Scribbet   Charcoal for drawing.

Scrogglings   Small, worthless apples left hanging on a tree after the crop is gathered.

Scrow   The sky.

Scrubbado (accent on *ba*)   "The itch."

Shab   To get rid of, to put something over on someone.

'sheart   A euphemistic shortening of *God's heart*, an oath.

Shiterow (long *i*)   A heron.

Shittle   Unstable, inconstant. From the Old English *sceotan* 'to run hastily'.

SHONGABLE   A tax on making certain shoes, in the 1400s.

SKIMMINGTON   A form of public ridicule practiced in the south of England to punish a husband for beating or betraying his wife. It consisted of a parade in which actors impersonating husband and wife rode through town on a donkey or in a cart beating each other with ladles or skimming spoons. See *riding the stang.*

SLIBBER-SAUCE   A nauseating concoction especially for medicinal purposes.

SLOOMY   Lazy, dull, sleepy.

SMELLSMOCK   A licentious man, a derogatory term for such priests.

SNAPSAUCE   Pilfering food; licking one's fingers.

SNAWK   To smell.

SNIRTLE   To snicker, to laugh quietly and mockingly.

SNOT   The burnt part of a candlewick, not a vulgar term in the fifteenth through seventeenth centuries.

SNOTTER-CLOUT   A pocket handkerchief.

SPARPLE   To scatter, spread about.

SPARROW-FART   Daybreak, very early morning.

SPERLING   A small fish, probably the European smelt, *Osmerus eperlanus;* a young American herring.

SPISS   Thick, dense.

SPITCHCOCK   Eel cooked with bread crumbs; quickly cut and cooked fowl, a quick dish for unexpected guests. From *despatchcock.*

SPIT-FROG   A small sword, a term of contempt.

SPITTLE   A hospital for lower-class indigents and lepers where they were housed but not necessarily cured.

SPOUSEBREAK   See *bedswerver*.

SPUDDLE   To assume airs of importance without reason; to make trifles seem important.

SQUECK   A disease affecting fowl.

SQUIDDLE   To waste time with idle talk.

SQUINT-A-PIPES   Slang for a squinting man or woman.

STEVEN   The voice, a loud outcry; a set time, appointment.

STOOP-GALLANT   Something that humbles the great and makes one a mere man; an early sixteenth-century name for a quick, fatal fever, the "sweating sickness."

STORGE (pronounced "stor'gee")   Natural love, especially of parents for their children. From the Greek *stergein* 'to love'.

STRAIGHT-FINGERED   Thoroughly honest, having fingers that won't bend to hold dishonest gains.

STREETMAN   An official appointed for the good government of the London streets.

SUGGILL   To beat black and blue; to defame.

SWARF-PENNY   Dues paid in commutation of the services of a castle guard.

SWELCHIE   A whirlpool. From the Old Norse *swelgan* 'swallow, devour' and the Old English *geswelg* 'abyss'.

SWERKED   To become troubled, gloomy. From the Old Saxon *swerkan.*

TABLINGHOUSE   A gambling house.

TAW-BESS   A slut, slattern.

TEAR CAT   A seventeenth-century term to criticize ranting actors who overdid their parts.

TEENFUL   Troublesome, irritating.

TENTERBELLY   A glutton.

THEEK   To cover a roof with straw thatch; to protect.

THEOW   A servant, slave.

THIBBLE   A stick for stirring porridge.

THIGGING   Begging.

THRING   Verb: to press, crush; noun: a throng.

THRIP   To snap one's fingers.

THRUNCH   Very angry, displeased.

TIDLIWINK   A tavern, possibly where the game of tid-liwinks arose; a *kidliwink.*

TINGLE-NAIL   The smallest kind of tack, a nail about one-quarter inch long.

TIPSYCAKE   Cake saturated with wine or liquor, stuck with almonds, and served with custard.

TIRLIRY-PUFFKIN   Light-headed, flighty woman, a flirt.

TITIVIL   A name for the devil, who steals words

dropped during the recitation of a service so the name can be used later against the offender; a knave, a tattler. From *Titivillus,* the devil, a word created by monks in mystery plays.

TITTUP   The canter of a horse, onomatopoetic from the sound of a horse's feet; to walk up and down in prancing movements; a forward woman, a hussy.

TRANTLES   Articles of little value.

TRUCKS   A game adapted from an Italian game like billiards. The English game had an upright form called a king placed at one end of table, to which one rolled balls over a board with thirteen holes in it.

TRUE-HEAD   Fidelity.

TRUNDLE-TAIL   A low-bred dog.

TURNGIDDY   Dizzy.

TUSHES   See *wang-tooth.*

TUTMOUTHED   Having protruding lips or a projecting lower jaw.

TUZZY-MUZZY   A nosegay of flowers. From the Old English *tus* 'cluster, knot'. Also *tisty-tosty.*

UG   Fear, dread.

UMBECAST   To consider or ponder. From the Old English *ymbe* 'around'; to surround, encircle.

UPSY   In the style of.

VASQUINE   A petticoat.

VECKE   An old woman.

VELLICATION   A twitching or convulsive movement.

VELVET HEAD   A term of contempt. From the head of a young deer, whose horns are covered with "velvet."

VENENATE   To poison.

VERME   A legendary fish from Ganges that was able to seize and destroy elephants.

VOIL   A town.

WAGHALTER   A rogue likely to swing in a gallows.

WALKING MORT   A grown-up unmarried whore, who often pretends to be a widow.

WALLYDRAIGLE   A worthless, slovenly woman.

WAM   A scar, cicatrix.

WANG-TOOTH   A molar. From the Old English *wang* 'to the side'. A *wang-tooth* is situated next to the *tushes* 'tusks'.

WELKIN   A sky with woolly clouds. From the Saxon *wealcan* 'to roll', *wolke* 'cloud', and the German *wolle* 'wool'.

WHEEPLE   An ineffectual attempt of a man to whistle loudly. An onomatopoetic term, from the low cheep of a bird.

WHIFLING   An insignificant creature.

WHIPPERGINNIE   An abusive term for a woman. The land of *whipperginnie* became a nickname for purgatory and a card game. Also *whip-her-jenny*.

WHISTERSNEFET   A blow to the ear. Also *whisterpoop*.

WHITELIVER   A coward.

WHOOPUBB   A hubbub.

WIDDERSHINS   Unlucky, prone to misfortune.

WIND-SUCKER   An envious, covetous person. A *yisser*. This term originally referred to a species of hawk that feeds on mice and hovers greedily, almost motionless, in the air over its prey. Chapman used the term to criticize Ben Jonson in the preface to his *Iliad*, saying, "There is a certain envious *wind-sucker* that hovers up and down, laboriously ingrossing all the air with his luxurious ambition."

WINK-A-PEEPS   Eyes.

WINX   To bray, as an ass.

WONG   Meadowlands, commons.

WOODNESS   Madness, insanity. From the Old English *wood* 'out of one's mind.'

WOUP   A hoop or ring, especially of plain metal, unset with stones.

WURP   A stone's throw; a glance of the eye.

XENODOCHIAL   Hospitable to strangers.

XIPH   A swordfish.

YARKEN   To prepare.

YCORE   Chosen, elect.

YEPSEN   Cupping the hands, and as much as the hands will hold. From the Old English *geap* 'open,' and *gowpen*, 'curved'.

YERD   To beat with a rod.

YERESYEVE   A gift given at the new year or upon taking office.

YETTER   A caster of metal.

YISSER   See *wind-sucker.*

YOUNGHEDE   A youth.

YUKY (pronounced *yooky*)   Itchy.

ZARF   A cup, especially one made of ornamental metal in Arabic countries. Also a cup-shaped holder for hot coffee.

ZEGEDINE   A drinking cup.

ZENDALET   A large, black, square, wool shawl folded into a triangle to be worn over the shoulders or on a wire frame on the head in eighteenth-century Venice. The word came to mean gondolas themselves, since the cloth trailed into the water.

ZOPISSA   An old medicinal application made from wax and pitch scraped from the sides of ships so coated as to harden and protect the metal.

ZUCHE   A tree stump.

fellowfeeling

Part 2

Tenderfeet & Ladyfingers

A COMPENDIUM OF BODY LANGUAGE

I like the words:
1. Wink-a-peeps. (all capit. letters)
   (eyes.
2. tipsy cake
3. Merry-Go-Sorry
   Hoddy Peak

Author's Note

The phrase "body language" means that the positions and postures which our bodies unconsciously assume reveal our attitudes without the need for words. The "body language" in this book is of a more literal nature. Many of the words and expressions we use without a moment's reflection contain references to different parts of the human body—and for good reason. Since one of the things we are most familiar with is our own body, it is natural that we project this preoccupation into other spheres. Such a notion is not new. Just as our ancestors measured by thumbs, hands, and feet, so we today incorporate body parts into our language. We apply "artery" to a road, "index," "spine," and "appendix" to a book, "mouth" to a river, and "neck" to a bottle. We cannot break the physical tie that links our bodies to our words, for when we speak of language itself, we are literally using our tongue, as the word "language" derives from *lingua,* the Latin word for tongue.

The proof of our preoccupation with our anatomy in language lies with the number of body words and idioms speakers of English have adopted over the years. We tend to spurn clichés because they are obvious. But it is their very obviousness that caused them to be born in the first place. Pause for a moment and consider a few graphic examples involving the human body. In these pages the reader will not find explanations of "elbowroom," "backbiter," "butterfingers," "give an arm and a leg," "eyes bigger than one's stomach," "a tongue-lashing," or of simple terms like "heady," "handy," "hearty," and "afoot" because they need no further explication. Their face value (!) is reason enough for their existence. Because language evolves with its exponents, what was fresh yesterday often becomes trite and is passed over in favor of new expressions. Overuse has indeed turned what was once original into cliché. But trite as many phrases have become, let us not forget that our language is being kept alive today by the descendants of those early observers of the associations between words and bodies.

The words and phrases explained in *Tenderfeet and Ladyfingers* are drawn from everyday use. Some readers may even label a few examples clichés, for the fine line between idiom and cliché varies according to the exposure a person has had to the particular expression. This collection is therefore the author's personal selection of those expressions that have more substance "than meets the eye." Although their definitions may be known to most, it is their unexpected histories, the reasons behind their being coined at all, their various uses in the past, and their underlying relationship to the human body that have all brought serendipitous delight to this author. Uncovering hidden surprises in the kinship between human anatomy and words is the author's intent. Serious scholars of etymology are invited to consult the bibliography for deeper study.

I wish to thank many people for their fellow-feeling on this project, the first being no less than William Shakespeare, whose words "Lend me your ears" inspired a verbal picture for this author long ago that fully developed only years later. Imagining Marc Antony's request being taken too literally and resulting in his being plied with a surfeit of ears made me conscious of the constant interplay between our bodies and our language. The thought of one good turn of phrase that incorporated a body part always reminded me of another and thereby reinforced my belief that a natural involvement with our physical being has had more impact on our language than most of us might realize at first.

Research has validated the theory; in talking with patient sympathizers, this word addict has learned new shades of meaning and acquired answers where only gaps used to be. I am indebted to supportive family members and enthusiastic friends as well as to generous historians, clergymen, and physicians for their contributions of time, information, and encouragement. To my editor I express gratitude for both her verbal assistance and her intuitive understanding of how best to give this corpus a refined shape.

Susan Kelz Sperling
Rye, New York
December 1979

In honor of two
word, mind, and body builders,
Drs. Siegfried and Paula Kelz,
and for
Allan, Matthew, Stuart, and Jane

The Head

The expression *to bite a person's head off* means to
speak harshly without listening to explanations or
excuses. As early as 1599 Thomas Nashe included
"to bite a man's nose off" in his *Oxford English Proverbs*. In the 1700s Susanna Centlivre, wife of Queen
Anne's head cook and the author of nineteen plays,
created a character who complained that a companion "snapp'd my nose off." The nose, because of
its size, position, and availability, is a logical choice
to bite. Although one still hears "to bite a person's
nose off," today the phrase more commonly appears
with the substitution of "head." Nose biting implies a minor fit of anger. Nothing surpasses the
image of biting off the entire head by delivering a
stentorian tirade that renders an opponent power-
less. It is literally capital punishment.

To be *head over heels,* or so involved as to be reeling,
may have originated with the ancient Roman poet
Catullus, whose Latin phrase *per caputque pedesque,*
"over head and heels," led to many variations. The
more reasonable terminology "heels over head" appeared in the 1300s and persisted even to 1864,
when Thomas Carlyle described in *Frederick the
Great* "a total circumgyration, summerset, or tum-
ble heels-over-head in the political relations of Europe." Over the years since Thackeray wrote in his

1840 *Paris Sketch-book,* "Why did you . . . hurl roy-alty . . . head-over-heels out of yonder Tuileries' windows?" the expression emerged with the head first and settled down into its current form.

To *hit* the *nail* on *the* head

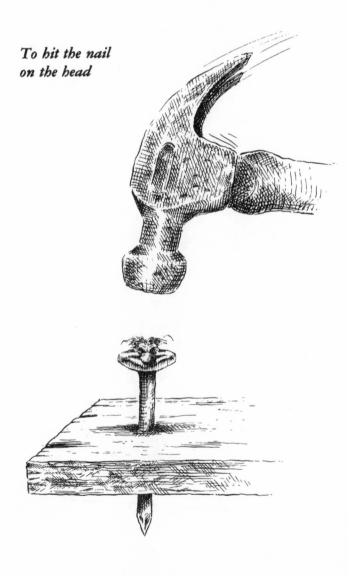

To hit the nail on the head, or to come to the right conclusion, has a number of counterparts in other languages. The French have the idiom *Vous avez frappé au but,* meaning "You have hit the mark." Italians say *Avete dato in brocca,* which translates literally into "You have hit the pitcher"—a reference to games of aim in which a pitcher served as a bull's-eye. The ancient Romans also had a phrase for it, namely *Rem acu tetigisti,* or "You have touched the thing with a needle," from the practice of probing the heads of sores with a needle.

The current application of *doubleheader* to mean two baseball games played in a row was borrowed from railroad terminology; the train of the same name uses two locomotives to pull twice the load. "Doubleheader" in carpentry identifies a door or window lintel made from two pieces of lumber held upright, placed next to each other, and then nailed or bolted together.

The popular saying *Two heads are better than one* is as old as the Bible, where it appears in the fourth chapter of Ecclesiastes. John Heywood, in his *Proverbs* (1546), states that "Two heddis are better than one," and Edmund Spenser asserts in *Mother Hubberd's Tale* (1591) that "Two is better than one head." As the quintessential statement of cooperation and fellowfeeling, it has remained relatively unchanged over the years. *Brewer's Dictionary of Phrase and Fable* offers a bit of homely psychology by perceiving the expression as the rhetorical an-

Two heads are better than one

swer to its own frequently added tag line, "Or why do folks marry?"

Kowtow, or "knock the head," is derived from the Chinese words *k'o,* to strike, and *t'ou,* the head. It was the custom from ancient times for Chinese people to bend down and touch the ground with the forehead when worshiping or paying respect to an esteemed member of the family. When this practice was carried to excess and became more form than feeling, "kowtow" earned its current connotation of fawning.

He didn't turn a hair, meaning that a person showed HAIR
little reaction, has as relatives the expressions
"didn't bat an eyelash" and "no sweat." Though it
appears to be current slang, "no sweat" is closely
akin to "not turning a hair," for both expressions
refer to breezing through a race without exerting
much effort, as exemplified by the horse that, well
ahead of its opponent, wins the race without getting its coat ruffled by wind or working up a sweat.
In 1798 Jane Austen made use of the idiom in
Northanger Abbey when she penned, "Hot! He had
not turned a hair till we came to Walcot church,"
while in 1897 Richard Blackmore wrote in *Dariel,*
"When I tried her with a lot of little dodges . . . she
never turned a hair—as the sporting people say."

To get in someone's hair means to annoy as pestily as
the lice and other insects that plagued the scalps of
our ancestors. A pithy remark in Shakespeare's time
was "Thou art ever in my beard," while an old Arab
saying invoked to insult or dismiss a nuisance declared, "May the fleas of a thousand camels infest
your armpits."

To let one's hair down implies behavior totally without pretense or affectation. The phrase calls to mind
the image of the exaggeratedly prim woman of early
films whose physical appearance was characterized
by dark, severe clothes and hair contained in a tight

bun, all of which pegged her for movie fans as a harsh, unfeeling character imprisoned by her own repression until a "good man" arrived on the scene to undo her hair and liberate her personality. Her prototype might well have been Grimm's fairy tale character Rapunzel, whose long tresses enabled not only the wicked witch but also the prince to have access to her tower-prison. When she learned of the prince's visits, the witch punished Rapunzel for both literally and figuratively letting her hair down by cutting her hair, casting her off into the desert, and indirectly causing the blinding of the prince. Pagans in earlier times observed the custom of not cutting the hair of their daughters until they were old enough to marry. When finally cut, the tresses were prepared as a sacrifice to the gods in return for fertility, health, and strength. The sexual connotation of a woman's offering her hair as a rite of passage to "escape" from virginity into maturity has brought about new interpretations of old tales and shed light on old rituals. The sex of the party shifts with the Biblical story of Samson, which illustrates the ancient belief that the strength and masculinity of a man were related to the length of his hair. Delilah literally made Samson her captive when she cut his locks, for he could not escape from the Philistines until his hair grew longer and his strength returned. Wearing the hair long and releasing one's emotions through music has led to the term *long-hair* (see page 132).

The hair of the dog that bit you may seem unrelated to the human body, but therein lies the inherent capriciousness of an idiom, for the situation that calls for the hair of the dog is human indeed. Greek legend tells of the warrior Telephus, wounded by Achilles, whose injury proved incurable until the spear that caused the wound was brought to heal it. Achilles's spear was deemed to possess miraculous healing powers, for a special ointment containing rust from the weapon supposedly cured the wound. A more likely reason for the cure was the inclusion in the salve of a medicinal herb that Achilles favored and which bore the name *achillea* in his honor. In the 1700s one remedy for a dog bite consisted of covering the injury with an application made from cut and burned hairs of the offending dog. In Newfoundland the liver of the dog was applied, while in rural England the fat removed from a snake and then simmered supposedly cured its bite. Whether these practices helped is anyone's guess, but similar reasoning became the basis for recommending that a person with a hangover take some more of the hair of the dog or drink a bit more of the same liquor to alleviate the effects of being drunk. In his *Proverbs* John Heywood recorded the figurative use of the expression as early as 1546: "I pray the leat [they let] me and my felow haue a heare of the dog that bote us last night." If one is inclined to scoff at the ignorance of our ancestors, one might also pause to consider the fact that our research into immunology today is based on similar principles.

It was physically impossible *to split hairs* until, in the nineteenth century, technology advanced to the

point of developing machines sophisticated enough to slice through matter as thin as one-two-hundredth of an inch, the width of a hair. The image of such fine cutting remains amazing enough for this idiom—which means to argue to a ludicrous degree over minuscule matters—to make sense still. Charles Darwin, however, extolled the virtues of inquisitive hairsplitters in his *Life and Letters* of 1887: "It is good to have hair-splitters and lumpers. Those who make many species are the splitters."

The erroneous spelling of *hairbrained* is more widespread than the correct version "harebrained." The term, which describes a person who has no more sense than a hare, was coined in the sixteenth century when orthography was not an issue. Both spellings have existed for a long time. Shakespeare used the term in *Henry VI, Part I:* "Let's leave this town; for they [the English] are hair-brained." Lewis Carroll named his character the March Hare because of the animal's wild and foolish conduct, especially during the March mating season.

A hair-raising experience, one in which fear causes one's hair to rise, is due to the normal physical response to fear called the pilomotor reaction. The Biblical Job recalled such an occurrence: "Then a spirit passed before my face that made the hair of my flesh to stand up." Even a bald person can speak of having the hair on his head stand on end; nerve ends cause the same sensations under the skin and hair follicles of the scalp as everywhere else. This universal condition, the inspiration for common expres-

A hair-raising experience

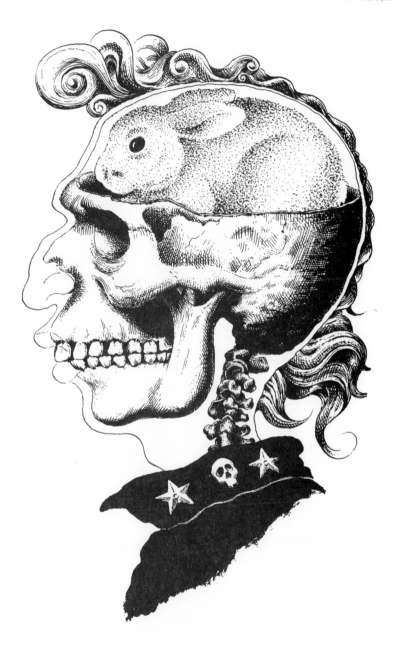

sions like "spine-tingling," "That made my flesh creep," and "It made my skin crawl" also gave rise to the modern slang terms "creepy" and "hairy," for all of these are simply restatements of how nerves react to unpleasant situations.

Particularly intriguing is the expression *as crafty as a red-haired person.* Judas, whose hair supposedly was red, is responsible for this attribution of untrustworthiness to redheads. Moreover, in medieval times, the fat of a dead red-haired person was in great demand as an ingredient in making poisons. George Chapman, an English dramatist, alluded to this practice in his 1607 *Bussy d'Ambois,* in which he wrote that flattery, like the plague

> Strikes into the brain of man,
> And rageth in his entrails when he can,
> Worse than the poison of a red-haired man.

EAR The superstition that a person is the subject of conversation if his *ears are burning* may not be as foolish as some may think. Pliny held that guardian angels touched the subject's right ear if the talk was favorable and the left if it wasn't, thereby bringing a message of cheer or a warning. Chaucer wrote in *Troylus and Cryseyde,* "And we shall speak of thee somewhat, I think, when thou art gone, to make thine ears glow." Tingling ears should be distinguished from itching ears, a phrase referring to the person who enjoys hearing about scandal and gossip.

The walls have ears is an expression truer than one might imagine. The observation that one's words can be overheard when one least expects it has a glorious past. In ancient Greece, Dionysius, the tyrant ruler of Syracuse, held prisoners in a cave made of rock that was over seventy feet high and two hundred feet deep and nicknamed "Dionysius's ear" because of its ear-shaped entrance and sound-conducting quality. An underground passage connecting the cavity to the palace enabled Dionysius to listen from far away to the conversations of his captives without their knowledge. A similar room nicknamed "the whispering gallery" was cut from solid rock beneath Hastings Castle in England. Furthermore, upon moving into the Louvre, Catherine de' Medici, suspicious of plots against the state, had rooms connected to her own chambers by hidden channels called *auriculaires,* literally "ear-witnesses," so that she could overhear what was being said in other rooms.

A dog-eared book contains ragged pages—the result of the reader's constantly folding down the edges to make bookmarks. These resemble the turned-over ears of most dogs. The term "dog's-eared," recorded as early as 1659, was also used to describe the frayed pockets of trousers.

Earmarking was an early form of copyright. From the 1500s on, farmers in England notched the ears of their sheep and cattle as a means of identification. But the practice of boring holes in people's ears to establish ownership is much older, as revealed in Ex-

The walls have ears

odus 21:6: "His master shall bore his ear through with an awl and he shall serve him for ever." This custom also became a sign of loyalty in Biblical times, for if a servant after six years of duty did not wish to be freed he could request that his ears be drilled as sign of his voluntary service. This custom gradually lost favor, and earmarking became a sign of punishment befitting the crime of stealing or altering the mark of another business person. Guilty offenders suffered the indignity of having their own ears notched while they were exhibited in the pillory. The practice of branding superseded earmarking when attempts at protecting property became more complex. The terms "brand name" and "trademark" entered our vocabulary when laws ensured the right of a tradesperson to place a unique mark on the goods he had made as a means of preventing others from stealing his ideas.

To face the music, or to accept the consequences of FACE one's actions, may derive from the early days of the American military, when a soldier dishonorably discharged had to stand at attention in front of a line of drummers and be literally drummed out of his rank. Another possible explanation is that mounted horses have to be trained to stay in formation, facing front, when a band plays. And lastly, a stage performer obviously has to overcome his nervousness and be prepared to face the audience seated beyond the orchestra pit. The phrase was first recorded thus in the *Worcester Spy* of September 22, 1857: "A strong determination to face the music is everywhere manifested." In his book *Americanisms* of 1872, Schele deVere quoted James Fenimore Cooper as having said, "Rabelais' unpleasant 'quarter' is by our more picturesque people called 'facing the music.' "

It is difficult *to keep a poker face* when a situation calls for some reaction. Like the poker player who tries to look impassive in order to conceal his elation over a particularly good hand of cards, someone who doesn't wish to give away his true feeling must appear almost expressionless and therefore "poker-faced." The phrase may also be associated with the rigidity of a poker, the metal rod used to stir a fire.

BROW   *To browbeat* an opponent is to use one's eyebrows as weapons. The expression has been in use since the 1500s, with a curious episode in its history occurring in the 1800s. During cross-examinations in British courts, prosecutors were restrained by law from assuming arrogant poses, looking down contemptuously, or even knitting their brows, since such actions put them at risk of being found in contempt of court for bullying witnesses into submission.

The apple of one's eye, a term for the object of a per-   EYE
son's affections, stems from the ninth century,
when the Anglo-Saxon word *aeppel* meant both
apple and eye. Since then, physiologists have proved
that when one looks at a particular person or object
for which he has special feeling, his pupils automatically dilate. That precious person or object fills up
each round pupil of the viewer's eyes and, by occu-
pying his total vision, figuratively becomes the
apple of his eye. He feels at that moment almost as
protective of that special love object as he does of
the precious pupils themselves. The author of Psalm
17 used the metaphor "Keep me as the apple of the
eye, hide me under the shadow of thy wings." A bit
of folk etymology maintains that our forefathers,
unacquainted with the sophisticated concept of
light refraction, mistook the reflected image a person saw of himself when he looked into another
person's eyes to be a precious little doll inhabiting
the *aeppel* itself. The Latin word *pupilla*—a diminutive of *pupa,* or girl—first meant that doll-like figure
living within the eye. Only later was the word applied to the actual pupil.

The Pinkerton Detective Agency of Chicago was
the first *private eye* organization, offering for hire not
public employees, but, for the sake of discretion,
private detectives. Allan Pinkerton, the founder of
the agency, was born in Glasgow, Scotland, in 1819
and traveled in 1842 to Illinois, where he became
first a detective and in 1861 both bodyguard to
Abraham Lincoln and head of the Secret Service for
the duration of the Civil War. When he established

his agency of private "i's" or "investigators," he adopted the logo of a huge, protective, and intimidating eye intended to convey the image of total surveillance. The term spread in popularity as a pun on both the discreet "i" and the all-seeing "eye."

To give someone the evil eye has a fascinating history. Believers of witchcraft held that certain people possessed the evil eye, or the power of putting a hex upon another person with just a glance. Spitting over one's shoulder in the hopes of blinding the demonic eye was a way of overcoming this curse, which was known as "eyebiting" about three hundred years ago. The origin of this superstition goes back to the Romans, who called the power to put someone under a spell *fascinatio*. To protect themselves from the devils in their midst, ordinary folk adorned themselves and their cattle with amulets specially designed to deflect the power of the evil eye; a child wore a particular amulet called a *fascinum*. Perhaps the Gershwin brothers had this bit of history in mind when they wrote of the spell of "Fascinating Rhythm."

The epithet *green-eyed monster,* meaning jealousy, gained in popularity with Shakespeare, who gave Iago these words in *Othello:* "O, beware, my lord, of jealousy! It is the green-eyed monster, which doth mock the meat it feeds on." Like the green-eyed wild animal that needs the prey it stalks, a jealous person both envies and despises the object of his ambivalent feelings. The linking of green eyes with the sickness of jealousy is also due to the early association of green with actual illness, for it is known that a faulty liver will cause a person's skin and eyes to appear greenish yellow. A faulty conclusion pertaining to green eyes, however, was the basis for the following expression.

To see with a jaundiced eye means to regard a person with a scorn that attempts to disguise envy. According to James G. Frazer in *The Golden Bough,* the ancient Romans had a remarkable cure for jaundice sufferers: the victim paid a high fee for the opportunity to look directly into the large eyes of the sacred stone-curlew bird. If the bird returned his stare, the sick man was considered healed, for the curlew supposedly possessed the power to draw out the affliction through its own golden-green eyes. So precious and revered were these birds that their owners kept their cages covered most of the time to prevent jaundice victims from sneaking a look and being cured without payment. Pliny recounts a further custom of assigning the Greek word for jaundice to a more common bird and then slaying the bird, thereby eradicating the illness. In the seventeenth century the word "jaundice" itself meant jealousy. While it is true that the liver dysfunction called jaundice causes the white of the eye to look slightly yellow, medical findings have proved false the early belief held even into the 1800s that people with jaundiced eyes actually see all things as yellowish green and therefore have a sour outlook on the world.

Here's mud in your eye!

The toast *Here's mud in your eye!* literally means "Bottoms up!" When a glass of wine or other liquid is quickly inverted for drinking, the sediment collected at the bottom can slide directly into the drinker's eye. In medieval times what collected at the bottom was usually the remains of ignited bits of toasted bread floating in the cup of spirits that a gallant youth dared to drink in honor of his loved one. His defiance of the danger of fire during this ritual, known as "flap-dragon," was the origin of the tribute we call a toast, even though the burning sops of toast were removed long ago. Nowadays when the expression is spoken with a sneering undertone, it usually means "I hope you get what you deserve." One story behind this snide connotation comes from horse racing. If two riders are competing on a muddy track, the rider of the second horse might very well be the victim of the other's strategy to get mud splashed into his face.

To pull the wool over someone's eyes, or to trick or surprise someone, originated when it was the fashion for gentlemen to wear fancy wigs made of "wool"—at one time a synonym for hair, as it derived from the Latin word for hair, *villus,* and the Old English *wull.* Practical jokers and robbers would surprise the wearer of a wool wig from behind by pushing the wig down over his eyes so that he couldn't see. An expression of similar extraction is "to hoodwink," the natural result of a sixteenth-century definition of "wink," to have one's eyes closed. A person wearing the kind of hood that was in style then was also easy prey for pranksters who could simply knock the hood down from in back of the wearer and, in so doing, cover his eyes. In the 1570s the game we refer to today as "blindman's buff" was called "hoodwink." A further example of deception gave rise to the following expression.

To *throw dust in one's eyes* means to dupe or mislead a person deliberately so that he cannot see things clearly. In the battle of Honein, the prophet Muhammad supposedly threw dust in the air to confuse his enemies, and this apparently successful tactic led to a new turn of phrase.

To *have one's eyes peeled* or *skinned* means to be on the alert. It comes from the idea of opening one's eyes so wide that the lids or "skins" are drawn up to their maximum height, leaving the eye looking as though the lids have been removed—or like a peeled orange. The idea behind the term is undoubtedly that eyes without lids would never miss even the slightest action. But since blinking is necessary to provide the eyes with essential moisture, the impossibility of maintaining a lids-up position for long gave rise to the expression. In 1889 a lexicographer named John Farmer defined "keeping the eyes peeled" in his *Americanisms* as "to keep a sharp look out; to be careful. A variation of 'to keep one's eyes skinned.'"

The term "cockeyed" generally applies to a situation that is muddled and out of kilter. A person *with a cockeyed look* shuts one eye, squints with the other, and tilts his head when assuming a doubting, inquisitive look, as if to ask "Huh?" His pose resembles that of a rooster who cocks, or tilts, his head and moves his eyes from side to side when strutting. In the 1800s cocking the eye did not mean that the posture was skewed out of its usual alignment, as it does today, but that one had a knowing look as self-assured, or cocksure, as a rooster.

A person *with a walleyed stare* looks as though he can see out of both sides of his eyes at the same time. The condition is caused by having an unusually large white section of the eye. With more white showing, the cornea looks off-center and the iris appears skewed off toward the side of the head. While today the expression applies to a person with an unfocused look, in the 1600s this glare was interpreted as a sign of the devil at work, and any person who possessed the trait was shut away as deranged. The only connection with a wall is tangential at best, and is relevant only if the subject happens to be leaning against one, for the phrase comes from the Middle English *wald-eyed,* a corruption of the Icelandic *vald eygthr,* or "having a beam in the eye," since the Old Norse *vagl* means beam.

Someone who *didn't bat an eyelash* maintained his equilibrium when others would have become flustered or embarrassed. The phrase comes from a seventeenth-century definition of "bat," fluttering or lowering the eyes. In 1615 Simon Latham discussed its particular application to the hawk in his *Falconry:* "To bat is when a hawk fluttereth with her wings either from the pearch or the mans fist, striuing as it were to flie away." Both "abate" and the "bate" of the phrase *with bated breath* (see page 32) are related to this early definition of "bat" that in the above phrase served to describe a truly unflappable person.

NOSE *To count noses* and *to pay through the nose* are closely related. A horse dealer usually counts by noses as a cattle dealer counts by heads. When applied to people the expression "to count noses" refers to taking attendance or calling for votes. The connection between the two expressions goes back to the ninth century, when the Danish conquerors of Ireland imposed the Nose Tax on the peasants. They took a census (by counting noses), levied op-

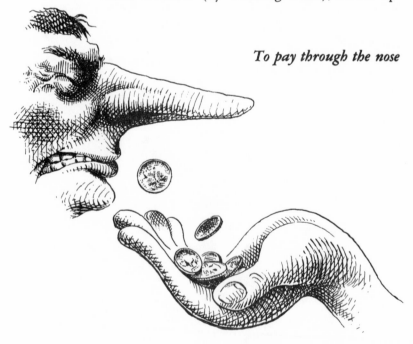

To pay through the nose

pressive sums on their victims, and forced them to pay by threatening to have their noses actually slit. Thus arose the slang phrase "being bled for money." By the seventeenth century the expression "to pay through the nose" was part of criminal argot, and whether thieves knew it or not, their use of the slang term "rhino" for money stemmed from the Greek word for nose, *rhinos.* Later the expression became a metaphor for having to pay excessively until it hurt. Arnold Bennett wrote a fitting limerick:

> There was a young man from Montrose,
> Who had pockets in none of his clothes;
> > When asked by his lass
> > Where he carried his brass,
> He said, "Darling, I pay through the nose."

To cut off one's nose to spite one's face, or to punish oneself while getting back at someone else, first appeared in the twelfth century in the Latin writings of Peter of Blois, a French churchman who served under Henry II of England. In 1796 Francis Grose wrote in his *Classical Dictionary of the Vulgar Tongue,* "He cut off his nose to be revenged to his face. Said of one who, to be revenged of his neighbor, has materially injured himself."

A person who finds his *nose out of joint* is annoyed at either a change in plans or simply not getting his own way. Barnaby Rich used this very old expression when he wrote in 1581 in *His Farewell to Mil-*

itarie Profession, "It could bee no other then his owne manne that has thrust his nose so farre out of ioynte." A century later Samuel Pepys was also fond of this phrase for being piqued, and around 1895 Cape Codders used a version of it in the colloquialism "having your nose broke."

On the nose, a modern idiom for being right on time, owes its existence to live radio broadcasting. If a crew member wants to inform the person on the air that the timing of the program is on schedule, he conveys that message silently by placing a finger alongside his nose.

As most people know, *turning up one's nose* is a common way of showing contempt. The interesting point to ponder is *how* one goes about doing this. Wiggling the nose alone doesn't turn it up. Putting one's thumb on it and wagging the other fingers to literally "thumb one's nose" in mockery or to "make a long nose" is a coarse variation. The fact is that it is curling the upper lip that causes not only one's nose to turn up but also one's face to assume a look of total disdain.

A hard-nosed person is determined to see something through. The use of "hard" is especially apt, since it is not only the opposite of "soft" but also a synonym for "toughened." The hard-nosed person is the opposite of one with "a nose of wax," a sixteenth-century term for someone whose sense of conviction is as pliable as soft wax. The "toughened" sense comes from the tenacity of a dog on the scent. Although its nose may appear soft, a dog is inured to the pain that goes with persistently digging and sniffing until it finds its goal.

The person capable of telling a barefaced lie obviously is *cheeky* enough to be rude even when face-to-face with his adversary. In Dickens's *Bleak House,* published in 1852, one of the characters was upbraided "on account of his having so much cheek." Perhaps because "cheek" sounds somewhat British, "lip" is more frequently used today in such American slang expressions as, "Don't gimme any more of your lip!" Also interesting is the fact that to leer, another form of insult, means to "look over one's cheek," and derives from *lere,* the Middle English word for cheek, which in turn came from the Old English *hleor.* Perhaps the only response for a recipient of a cheeky remark or leer is to follow the advice in the next expression.

CHEEK

To turn the other cheek is synonymous with turning a deaf ear. The movement involved in both expressions is a turn of the head from one side to the other in order to deflect some form of visible or verbal abuse. This phrase, recommending diffidence when insulted or provoked, first appeared in the sixth chapter of the Book of Luke: "Unto him that smiteth thee on the one cheek offer also the other." Implicit is the lesson that the enemy is most easily disarmed by the unexpected response—here by an invitation to repeat his challenge, thereby showing him how little weight it carries.

LIP   The counsel *to keep a stiff upper lip,* meaning not to give in to weakness and cry, has an obvious parallel in "chin up." In his *down Easters* of 1833 John Easter wrote, "What's the use of boohooin? Keep a stiff upper lip, no bones broke—don't I know?" However, taking this advice to its extreme and never letting one's emotions show can lead to one's becoming a stiff upper lip, or a hard and unfeeling person. The Civil War added an interesting historical note to this expression when a certain powder cart was constructed with a built-in ridge that a soldier could best open with his upper front teeth. He had to keep a stiff upper lip so as not to waste time while the enemy advanced.

To pay lip service, or to be insincere in feeling though ardent in words, is as old as the Book of Isaiah, which conveys the same thought in other words: "Wherefore the Lord said, For as much as this people draw near me with their mouth, and with their lips to honor me, [they] have removed their hearts far from me. ..." In the 1500s "lip labor" meant vapid talk, applied particularly to repetition in prayer. About a hundred years ago the phrase "lip worship" meant the same kind of empty talk.

Like "hairbrained" *hairlip* should rightly be spelled harelip. The defect, caused by incomplete development of the upper lip and jaw, was so named because of its resemblance to the cleft lip of a rabbit. This condition has been mentioned in literature since the sixteenth century.

The lucky soul *born with a silver spoon in his mouth* is raised in luxury made possible by inherited wealth. A custom from the early 1700s verifies a literal interpretation of the phrase: during that period English godparents usually gave a christening gift of a set of twelve silver spoons decorated with figures of the apostles at the tops of the handles. In his *Scottish Proverbs,* published in 1721, James Kelly recognized the simple virtue of every person's working to support himself since "Every man is no [*sic*] born with a silver spoon in his mouth." In 1762 Oliver Goldsmith wrote in *The Citizen of the World* that "One man is born with a silver spoon in his mouth, and another with a wooden ladle."   MOUTH

Butter wouldn't melt in his mouth means that a person looks so innocent that he couldn't possibly be suspected of wrongdoing, let alone be found guilty. A somewhat curious expression that is over four hundred years old, its meaning becomes clear when one realizes that the human body generates different degrees of temperature to perform different functions. The person of whom it is said that butter wouldn't melt in his mouth assumes a countenance so placid and gentle that he appears to be incapable of producing even the small amount of heat necessary to melt as soft a substance as butter in his mouth. Some interpreters of this expression take it one step further and apply it to a rogue or scoundrel whose demeanor is consistently standoffish and cold.

The advice *don't look a gift horse in the mouth* means that one should accept a present, or even one's fate, graciously. Looking for more than what's there can lead to the disappointment of finding out that's all there is. The expression first appeared in an equivalent form in Latin about four hundred years ago, as did the phrase "straight from the horse's mouth." Both idioms originate from the fact that whatever one might hypothesize about the age of a horse, the truth is always to be found right in its mouth, for its teeth reveal its age.

One must avoid being too literal with the expression *to laugh on the wrong side of one's mouth* or one can become entangled in a silly debate over not only which side of the mouth is wrong but also whether or not a person laughs out of the sides at all. Originally the phrase meant to laugh in a forced way, perhaps by opening only one corner of the mouth just slightly. But since the 1700s the phrase has implied a quick change of expression from happy to sad as a result of an unexpected and unfortunate occurrence. It carries with it the cynical inference of a just comeuppance and is obviously kin to *the shoe is on the other foot* (see pages 98–99).

To laugh on the wrong side of one's mouth

One who is *mealymouthed* speaks as though he actually has meal, a flourlike substance with the consistency of cereal, in his mouth. His words, too, have as little substance as the thin Portuguese powder *enfarinhadamente*. But the phrase was not always derogatory, for it comes from an improper pronunciation of the Greek *melimuthos,* a word that combines *meli,* meaning honey, and *muthos,* meaning speech. One who talks in honeyed tones is sweet-speaking, but this attribute loses its appeal whenever the gentle, soft words either are without substance or are adopted to conceal true thoughts. In the past a nondistinctive, pale complexion was described as mealy. And Dickens used the expression to indicate the kind of character that was often called a "hairsplitter," one who minces or dissects things the same way that chunks of food can be chewed over and over until they become mush.

BREATH   The person who speaks *with bated breath* talks while his breathing is more subdued than usual. Terror, awe, anticipation, or another strong emotion restrains his normal pattern. As with the expression "He didn't bat an eyelash," the word "bate," like "abate," is another form of "bat," which means to lower or flutter and is not to be confused with the word "bait." Shakespeare used the phrase in *The Merchant of Venice* in 1596: "With bated breath, and whispring humblenesse."

Although *long in the tooth* may summon up the image of fangs, the expression has nothing to do with vampires. It merely recognizes the fact that as a person grows older, his teeth may appear to get longer, not because of new growth but because his gums are receding with age, thereby displaying the roots. The phrase was first applied to the horse, whose age can be readily determined by its teeth, but now is a popular way of saying "getting on in years." In 1978 a *New York Times* reviewer used the expression to criticize the choice of actors who were supposed to look like high school students in the motion picture *Grease.* A condition curious to rodents makes them naturally long in the tooth and adds another dimension to the phrase. The two exceptionally long, sharp incisors of each jaw would keep growing to the point of piercing the lining of the mouth were it not for the animals' filing them down by constantly gnawing.

A person with *buck teeth* has projecting front teeth. Although this condition usually pertains to the upper jaw, the expression comes from the fact that the male deer has front teeth only in its lower jaw. A thick pad of rough skin does the work of front upper teeth, as, for example, when it helps to tear leaves from trees for food. However, both the upper and lower jaws have back teeth with sharp tips for

TOOTH AND TEETH

A struggle in the teeth of the wind

chewing. It is therefore curious that the protrusion of a buck's teeth from only its lower jaw gave rise to a phrase commonly applied to humans yet seldom connected with animals.

By the skin of my teeth implies a narrow escape. The "skin" or enamel covering the teeth is as thin as the Biblical Job's margin of safety, as written in the nineteenth verse, "My bone cleaveth to my skin, and to my flesh, and I am escaped with the skin of my teeth."

A struggle in the teeth of the wind is a direct confrontation with an overwhelming problem or a show of strong defiance against all odds. The image is of a mocking, raging gust of wind—like that

pictured in fairy tales—blowing with all its might and sneering with teeth exposed at its victim, who, instead of being cowed, meets the challenge of overcoming his oppressor by facing the wind—or whatever else it might be—and fighting back. There may well be a connection between this phrase and "a biting wind." The phrase also conjures up a picture of the willing combatant baring his teeth during his physical or mental battle. In his *Epistles of Horace*, Alexander Pope wrote of one's intent "To strive with all the tempest in my teeth."

A person known to *lie through his teeth* has no compunction about telling falsehoods. But why through his teeth? The liar has to force himself to assume the calm demeanor that will conceal his duplicity. He attempts a hearty smile, baring but also often clenching his teeth as a means of controlling his emotions. Such a demonstration of body language is on a more bold and sinister level than simply speaking *tongue in cheek* (see pages 38–39). Whatever the motive, the earliest counterpart to the current phrase comes from the fourteenth-century work *The Romances of Sir Guy of Warwick:* "Thou liest amidward [between words] and therefore have thou maugreth [shown ill will]."

An experience that *sets one's teeth on edge* causes revulsion or pain. Locking one's jaws and taking a sharp breath are instinctive reactions on hearing the scrape of a fingernail or chalk on a blackboard, but these are mild aftereffects compared with those referred to by the prophet Jeremiah. In chapter 31, verse 29, of the Bible, he rebukes parents for their shortsightedness, warning them that their sins will cause their children to suffer: "The fathers have eaten a sour grape, and the children's teeth are set on edge." In *Henry IV*, Shakespeare warns that anything that jars one's sensibilities, such as "mincing Poetrie," will set one's teeth on edge.

The individual who *takes the bit in his teeth* ignores advice and goes his own way. He can become as unmanageable as a horse defying the rider's pull on its bit. To break in a horse, a rider places the horizontal bar of the bridle, known as the "bit," into the horse's mouth. When the rider tugs on one side of the reins, this bit pinches the cheek and conditions the horse to turn to the side on which it feels pressure. But if the horse puts the bit between its teeth, it does not feel the tug. It pays no attention to the wishes of the rider and runs off without being broken in. Like a defiant horse, a willful person can take the bit in his teeth—thereby going well beyond someone who merely turns a deaf ear.

To cut one's eyeteeth means to become worldly. By the time a child gets his permanent set of eyeteeth or canines—those that are third from the center in the upper jaw, so called because they resemble the pointed teeth of dogs—he is beyond babyhood and learning the ways of the world. Ralph Waldo Emerson recorded this phrase around 1870, but a British version from the 1700s carried a slightly different meaning. "To have one's eyeteeth" or "to have one's eyeteeth about one" meant to be on the alert for cheaters, especially in business affairs. It also applied simply to a person experienced in dealing with others—as obviously would be the case with anyone old enough to have had his eyeteeth for some time. These expressions led to the variation "to draw one's eyeteeth," meaning to pull them out, an uncommon but delightfully graphic way of showing one's desire to humiliate someone, to "take him down a peg." The more recognizable pledge "I'd give my eyeteeth" is a promise to part with something obviously difficult to give up and of great value.

TONGUE   The person figuratively *tongue-tied* speaks in a gar-
bled manner or not at all. His confusion or speech-
lessness is usually the result of a surprise or
momentary interruption in his normal behavior.
The physical malformation of a tied tongue is due
to an abnormal shortness of the membrane called
the *fraenum linguae* that connects the tongue to
the floor of the mouth. The British obstetrician
William Smellie suggested a cure in 1754:
"Tongue-tying is easily remedied by introducing
the forefinger into the child's mouth, raising up the
tongue, and snipping the bridle with a pair of scis-
sors." In 1905 the British newspaper *The Daily
Chronicle* applied the term to words more often
called tongue twisters: "There are names ... that
demand shortening, tongue-tiers such as Giggles-
wick which almost necessarily dwindles into Gil-
zick." It goes without saying that the British found
place names like Worcester, Gloucester, and Lei-
cester to be tongue-tiers as well and coped more easily with their contracted forms.

Words that are spoken *tongue in cheek* are voiced in a
tone that is disparaging, humorously flip, and somewhat self-conscious. The speaker deliberately draws
attention to his words as though wishing he could
tuck them away with his tongue into his cheek, to
garble them, or even to prevent their being heard.
In the delivery of such comments he often adopts
an affected, cute, or shy manner that might cause
the listener to question the sincerity of what he is
hearing. Matthew Arnold summed up this attitude,

the opposite of "straight from the heart," by describing a person as follows: "He unquestionably . . . knows that he is talking clap-trap, and, so to say, puts his tongue in his cheek."

To lick one's chops means to anticipate an enjoyable experience, usually the pleasure of food, by smacking the lips and licking the sides of the face around the mouth. "Chop" is a variation of "chap," an obsolete word for the bone of the jaw. In the plural, chops are the jaws that form the mouth. This phrase and its equivalent, "to lick one's lips," have both existed since the 1500s. During the seventeenth and eighteenth centuries the first phrase took a nasty turn and became synonymous with gloating over another person's misfortune. In twentieth-century jazz lingo, "to lick one's chops" means to tune up for a musical session.

CHOPS

A popular hair fashion at more than one time, the *spit curl* was a short curl of hair separated from the rest and plastered to the forehead with spit. Henry Wadsworth Longfellow first coined the expression "spite curl" in response to Blanche Roosevelt's unwillingness to learn the proper pronunciation of

SPIT

Spitting image

"forehead" despite the fact that he had composed the following rhyme especially for her:

> There was a little girl,
> And she had a little curl,
> Right in the middle of her forehead.
> When she was good,
> She was very, very good;
> And when she was bad,
> She was horrid.

The phrase *spitting image* has been in use since the 1800s, when the original "spit 'n image" was the correct spelling. Slurring the phrase caused the " 'n" or "and" to be understood as "ing." A person who is the spitting image of someone else—usually the child of his parent—resembles the other as closely as two drops of saliva from the same mouth. At an earlier time "spit" alone conveyed the same message. One might have said, "He is the very spit of his father," meaning that the likeness is so startling that it is as though the child had been spat out of his father's mouth. An alternate explanation is that blacks in the United States made use of the phrase in the belief that a child possesses the same spirit as, or a nature similar to, his parent. Turning "spirit" into the contraction "sp'i't" and adding "n" and "image" results in the above phrase, but the derivation involving ordinary spit is the more popular.

From Neck to Knuckles

If a person *sticks his neck out,* he is asking for it. "It" is trouble, the reward for meddling or for taking a risk. There is more than one realistic explanation for the phrase. The boxer who lifts his head, forgetting to tuck in his chin to his chest, truly "gets it in the neck." The butcher who stretches the neck of a chicken finds the right spot to decapitate it. Figuratively speaking, anyone whose neck is extended is liable to be severely hit with something, usually a stern reprimand or a lot of grief.

More than one section of the Bible uses the term *stiff-necked* in one form or another. Moses censures the Levites by saying, "For I have known thy rebellion, and thy stiff neck." Psalm 75 advises, "Speak not insolence with a haughty neck," and the books of Isaiah and Jeremiah also use the phrase. A stiff-necked person resembles a willful horse that keeps its neck rigid, ignoring the pull on its reins. It resists what is usually effective persuasion. The phrase has been in popular use since the 1500s as a synonym for obstinate, but it describes even more accurately the self-righteous snob whose very carriage speaks for itself.

The American slang term *necking,* which conjures up scenes of teenagers hugging and kissing in cars, has a colorful history. Its most recent usage obviously comes from lovers nuzzling each other's neck while embracing. Further back in history when Americans were settling the Old West, the word referred to the common procedure of tying a restless animal by the neck to tame him. Doing it for sport became a rodeo attraction. But the most illustrious form of necking took place during the Middle Ages when a man being knighted underwent the ritual called *accolata,* the physical hug around the neck, from the Latin *ac,* meaning "at" or "to," and *collum,* meaning "neck." After such an honor, from which the word "accolade" is derived, he received the customary kiss and tap with a sword on the shoulder.

SHOULDER The road sign *soft shoulder,* announcing that an unpaved road is upcoming on one side, is so named because a vehicle can slide into that dirt as easily as a head can sink into a yielding shoulder. Whoever gave the roadside such an evocative name (instead of, for example, a dull term like "unpaved side") deserves credit for language awareness, in contrast to the person who designed the misleading road sign with the word "slow" printed above the word "children." In some central and southern states the soft shoulder is called soft berm or berme, a term that derives from medieval times, when it was the name for the ridge between the edge of a moat around a castle and the fortress wall.

A person who speaks *straight from the shoulder* talks in as blunt a way as a fighter delivers a certain kind of punch. The boxer brings his fist up to his shoulder and aims straight at his opponent without crooking his elbow. This phrase is just one of a few that have entered everyday speech from boxing, others being "hitting below the belt," an indication of what is unfair or not allowed; "leading with the chin," or inviting a challenge or argument; and "taking it on the chin," which means stolidly receiving a blow, literal or figurative. In 1856 a British novelist and dramatist named Charles Reade called for candor in his treatise on social abuses *It Is Never Too Late to Mend:* "No! give me a chap that hits out straight from the shoulder. . . ."

It is easy to spot someone with *a chip on his shoulder,* since such a person would look as eager for a challenge as did players of a game of distance and skill popular in the United States in the 1800s and from which this phrase derives. Under the rules of the game, one person would challenge an opponent to knock a block of wood from his shoulder—whether with an instrument or by hand is unknown—and would then measure the distance the block traveled. Perhaps as this game grew more heated, the expression earned its quarrelsome connotation. There is also a theory that the phrase originated among American lumberjacks, particularly those working on the ground below a tree being felled. Perhaps the possibility of having heavy chips of wood fall on their shoulders at any time caused many to adopt a sour outlook. Before "shoulder" entered the phrase, a sixteenth-century adage admonished, "Hew not too high lest chips fall in thine eye." In time the warning became a dare. A person would show off his fearlessness by daring to look high into a tree being cut down without flinching at the sight of falling chips.

The shoulder of the current expression *to give someone the cold shoulder* is not the same kind of shoulder that people offered in medieval days. After a hard day of knightly endeavors, knights could always anticipate receiving a hot meal at any abode. People warmly offered their homes and food, having prepared extra meals of lamb and beef just in case visitors chanced by. When the Middle Ages ended and customs changed, unexpected guests found fewer doors open to them and could consider themselves fortunate to be given even cold meat, usually a shoulder of mutton. If they arrived well after dark, they would be lucky if they could "kiss the hare's foot"—that is, nibble on anything at all. The roasted shoulder of mutton that used to be a symbol of hospitality itself eventually turned into the leftovers that people were reluctant to share and, later, into the figurative cold shoulder offered by people who resent intrusions. By the 1800s the phrase "give the cold shoulder" was firmly entrenched as a popular way of describing how one should treat a person with contempt or indifference so that he will go away. The French have a similar expression, *faire grise mine à,* which means " to give someone a gray look."

To give someone the cold shoulder

The advice *keep your shoulder to the wheel* suggests putting in extra effort to solve a problem and not giving up in despair. During the building of the pyramids, it was probably common practice literally to position one's shoulder to the wheel. One of Aesop's fables told of a man whose cart got stuck in mud. When he called to Hercules for help, Hercules reprimanded him for not applying the weight of his own shoulder more vigorously to the stuck wheel. The phrase easily passed from the literal sphere into the metaphorical because of the universality of its message. After great exertion, one's desire to keep plugging naturally increases when success is in sight. Such a drive for completion is implied in the words Andrew Marvell wrote in 1678 in *Growth Popery:* "If it had hitherto seemed to go up-hill, there was a greater cause to put the whole shoulder to it."

The easily understood expression *to shoulder a burden* obviously comes from the training of oxen and other animals to carry heavy burdens on their shoulders. But, interestingly enough, this way of saying that one feels the weight of a big responsibility on one's mind also recalls an obsolete English custom called the "shoulder-feast," a dinner given after a funeral just for those people who carried the coffin.

———

The popular slang expression *It's the pits* is too new ARMPIT
for its derivation to have been documented. One
could logically assume that this crude way of saying
that something is of the lowest rank may have come
from the term that describes both deep holes in the
ground and the part of the fruit that one naturally
rejects. Both of these etymologies could be valid, as
could a more graphic explanation that has ties to
the body theme. After a heroin addict has injected
the drug into almost every available vein, he is des-
perate to locate any spot not yet covered with needle marks and stoops to his last resort, the armpits,
the maximum low. Similarly, the nonaddict whose
mood goes "down to the pits" feels that he too has
hit bottom.

Holding a person *at arm's length* simply means ARM
keeping him at a distance, not wanting to get involved. Attorneys use the phrase to apply to any
deal in which two parties negotiate terms that are
fair and agreeable to both. The informal connotation of deliberately keeping away from someone
does not enter here; as used by lawyers, the phrase
applies only to a straightforward business arrange-
ment. The opposite is a "sweetheart deal," in which
one party does a favor for another without expecting anything in return.

Although *up in arms* may evoke the image of a
crowd of people waving their arms in the air, the

*Up **in** arms*

phrase actually refers to man's readiness to find
means of defense stronger than his first weapons, his
arms. Both crude and man-made armaments are
simply extensions of the arms designed to provide
further protection. A group of soldiers up in arms is
fully fortified to fight. In times past, French people
rallied their troops to arm themselves by spreading
the urgent message *"À l'arme!"*—or, in English,
"Go to your arms!"—from which arose the English
word "alarm," a signal of any emergency. Since then

the expression has lost its strict military references and now aptly describes a person who is indignant or agitated enough to pick a fight.

Suggesting that someone should use a little *elbow grease* is another way of saying he should work harder, even to the point of getting sweaty. This current meaning is rooted in the seventeenth century, when the term "elbow grease" actually meant sweat. Perhaps the two were synonymous because the perspiration or "grease" that a person worked up was a reliable measure of how energetically he moved his elbows to rub, polish, or accomplish any work that required physical exertion. In 1672 Marvell distinguished between two types of people when he wrote, "Two or three brawny fellows in a corner, with mere ink, and elbow grease, do more harm than an [*sic*] Hundred systematical Divines with their sweaty preaching." Writing in *Thackeray* in 1879, Trollope waxed rhapsodic for would-be writers: "Forethought is the elbow-grease which a novelist,—or poet, or dramatist—requires."

ELBOW

Whether preplanned or accidental, a *handicap* holds a person back. In the fourteenth century a game called "Newe Faire," later known as "hand i' cap,"

HAND

was played by two people who agreed beforehand to trade their goods, with the help of an umpire who decided on the fairness of the transactions. Each player first put the same amount of money into a cap held in the umpire's hand. One player then offered to exchange an article for something offered by the other player. The umpire judged both articles and determined how much more money had to be added to make the trade fair. At that point both players made the gesture of going into their pockets for coins. If both drew out some more money, then they could make the exchange final, and the money in the cap would go to the umpire. If neither offered more money, then the umpire got the previously pledged money and no trade was completed. If only one player took out money, he won the money in the cap and no goods were exchanged. Pepys commented on the game in 1660: "Among the pleasures some of us fell to handycapp, a sport that I never knew before." Horse racing adopted some of these practices in the seventeenth century, and when the sport expanded, so did the role of the umpire. Entrants would draw lots from a cap held by the umpire in order to determine which horse would be placed closest to the rail, which was the most desirable position. The umpire would also assess the different weights of the horses and decide what additional weight the favorite had to carry to make all contestants equal. The owners would then also draw from a cap to vote on whether the race was on or off. As the scope of sports grew wider, "handicap" took on a broader application and came to mean the penalty or forfeit a given player would carry in order to avoid having an advantage over the other players. Golfers today close that gap by starting out with strokes already added to their game. In other activities any added reasonable condition that makes a leading contestant's efforts more difficult is called a handicap; if he can overcome that drawback, he emerges the winner. The reason for applying the word to people with disabilities is apparent, although the term's derivation is not.

Handsome had many more meanings a few hundred years ago than it does today. In the 1400s it meant "easy to deal with" or "easy to handle." From the 1500s to the 1800s it also meant "ready at hand" or "handy," as well as "considerable" (as applied to amounts), "proper," "fair," and the contemporary "pleasing to look at." One can link its most popular definition today with its earliest meaning if, diehard romantics excepted, one accepts that what is easiest to deal with is also the most pleasing.

To give a person a *left-handed compliment* is to leave him wondering whether he has received a compliment at all. The ambiguity of such a remark is part of a long history of attributing mystical qualities to things "left." Our ancestors observed that for most people the right hand is the stronger of the two, and a right-handed person finds it awkward to use his left hand. The Anglo-Saxon word *lef* actually meant "weak," not the opposite of "right." Consequently, at some distant point in the past the majority (i.e., right-handed people) concluded that left-handed people possessed a type of demonic magic that caused the deviation. Therefrom arose the superstition of avoiding anything pertaining to "left." Even the Latin and French words for "left," *sinister* and *gauche,* reveal how "left" earned a bad connotation in more than one language. The ancients dreaded omens that were visible on the left side and believed that bad luck would descend upon a house which a person entered into or departed from with the left foot first (see *to put one's best foot forward,* pages 96–97). By the Middle Ages people translated their fear into magical and religious customs. Because they believed that the devil always lurked just behind one's left shoulder, superstitious people threw salt or resorted to spitting over that shoulder to extinguish the power of his omnipresent evil eye (see *to give someone the evil eye,* page 18). The traitorousness of Judas, who supposedly sat *ad sinistram,* or to the left, of Jesus at the Last Supper, served to confirm the equation of "left" with evil. In medieval art souls that were damned were positioned to the left of Christ. From the conviction that those who sat to the right of the Lord—*qui sedet ad dexteram Patris*—were in a position of strength arose the concept behind the phrase *a right-hand man,* a trustworthy, eager-to-serve, confidential assistant. A knight's bodyguard purposely situated himself to the right of his leader. By keeping his own right hand free, he was always ready to reach for his sword and defend his knight. By the 1600s "right-hand man" referred to the cavalryman who was stationed to the right of the line and given a great deal of responsibility. The phrase also easily applied to other spheres, as the writer John Stephens illustrated in his 1615 *Satyrical Essayes:* "A Lawyers simple Clarke is his Masters right hand, if hee bee not left-handed." As "right" prevailed, so did the weak, invalid aspects of left-handedness. A "left-handed marriage" became a term for one binding in common law only. Conversely, one account that links "left" with good luck and strength comes from the Incas' reverence for their great left-handed chief, Lloque Yupanqui, whose name means left-handed and whose qualities they emulated. Modern research into the dominant centers of the brain may provide explanations, but long-standing expressions demonstrating our folkloric roots are not easily dismissed.

Our interpretation of *high-handedly* has changed since the days of its inclusion in the Bible. The Book of Numbers recounts that ". . . on the morrow after the passover the children of Israel went out with a high hand in the sight of all the Egyptians." This Biblical reference to a high hand symbolized God's protection and accounted for the term's original meaning, "triumphantly." A shade of arrogance colors the term when people already in control—those figuratively or literally holding their hands high—take advantage of their position of dominance by flaunting their absolute power. The variation "keeping an upper hand" so as to be one step ahead of the opposition suggests an offensive, intimidating tactic.

It is not a compliment today for a person to be told that he writes in *a fine Italian hand,* for it means that he is a sly manipulator who uses surface appearances to cover his deceit. The history of this phrase dates back to the fifteenth century, when church officials kept records in a style of writing called *cancelleresca* that was both ornate and graceful and opposite in feeling to the Gothic style of northern Europe. As time went by, laymen and politicians—usually crooked ones—adopted the fancy script to falsify documents. Unfortunately for the term, the reputations of the not-so-innocent politicians, plotters, and other unsavory characters lent a sardonic twist to a seemingly inoffensive remark.

The expression *a bird in the hand is worth two in the bush* is included here not to clarify its well-understood advice that holding on to what is secure is sometimes wiser than taking risks, but to list the many delightful variations this saying went through until it reached its present form. Its first recorded mention dates from 1470, when people said, "Betyr ys a byrd in the hand than tweye in the wode." Two citations from 1530 are known, one from the *Book of Nurture* suggesting that a bird in the hand is worth "ten flye at large" and another from the *Commonplace Book* that states that one in hand is worth "three in the wode." In 1546 Heywood continued to favor the use of ten as a proper figure, while in 1678 a writer named Ray raised the number to one hundred. It was Skelton, in 1620, who changed "wode" (or "wood") to "bush." From the late 1600s on, the phrase has remained fairly stable.

The custom of *shaking hands on it* to consolidate an agreement goes back centuries. The application of the hand has always had significance; for example, in Roman times a slave owner culminated the formal contract of purchasing slaves by ceremoniously putting his hand on each one's head. Moreover, if a son wished to set out on his own when he came of age, he could be released from his father's hold only if he entered into the ritual called *emancipatio*. The father would grasp his son's hand and then let it go three times, thereby literally emancipating him, since "emancipate" derives from the Latin words *e*, which means "out of" or "from," and *manus*, which means "hand." In feudal times a vassal pledged loyalty by putting his hands into those of his overlord while taking an oath, and it was from this practice that both the graphic (and now obsolete) word "hand-band," which describes a covenant between parties, and the phrase "to strike hands," or make a contract, arose. One must also not dismiss the historical importance of shaking hands as a self-protective measure. Upon meeting and departing, knights would offer their hands to each other in a seemingly chivalrous gesture that also served to reassure both men that neither would reach for his sword. Today the simple gesture of shaking hands to show welcome and friendship is rooted in the importance ascribed in the past to the giving of one's hand. The act was so binding a promise, such an avowal of one's honor, that Proverbs warned: "Senseless is the man who gives his hand in pledge, who becomes surety for his neighbor."

Pontius Pilate is the most notorious person to have *washed his hands of a matter.* The Book of Matthew recounts "When Pilate saw that he could prevail nothing, but that rather a tumult was made, he took water, and washed his hands before the multitude, saying I am innocent of the blood of this just person: see ye to it." Although the phrase may have been intended to imply that the point in question could be easily dismissed, it has acquired a taint of suspicion. Shakespeare's Lady Macbeth unquestionably stands for the person who refuses to assume guilt, as symbolized by the "damned spot" she tries to wash away.

To win hands down means to win easily. As with "he didn't turn a hair" and "no sweat," the phrase alludes to horse racing. A jockey who sees that he is in the lead need not worry about prodding his horse, so he relaxes his hold on the reins by letting his hands drop. Conversely, keeping a firm grip on the reins explains the phrase "out of hand," since a horse that doesn't feel the authority of its master can easily go out of control.

PALM   Someone about *to grease a person's palm* is ready to offer money as a bribe in return for having that person grant him a favor. A very old expression, it is a translation of the medieval French phrase *oindre la paume à quelqu'un.* Some Britishers euphemistically refer to the practice as "a tip for Mr. Palmer." The slightly puzzling element here is the use of the word "grease," but the confusion is eliminated when one visualizes the physical act of slipping money furtively into another person's hand. To cover up his intent, the giver would conceal the bribe in his palm and casually reach for the other's hand in what would look like a gesture of friendship. Both his nervousness and his need to hold the other person's hand long enough to transfer the money could produce sweat, the "grease" of the expression.

The person who *has an itching palm* is expecting to have it greased (see above). The most well-known instance of a person's willingness to take a bribe is found in Act IV of *Julius Caesar,* in which Brutus rebukes Cassius for his greed. After Cassius complains that Brutus has condemned one of Cassius's friends for taking a bribe, Brutus says, "Let me tell you, Cassius, you yourself are much condemned to have an itching palm." Since Shakespeare's time the phrase has taken on added dimensions. One superstition holds that a palm which suddenly starts to itch is an indication that the subject will get money. Folklore goes so far as to suggest that an itching left palm means that a person will receive money, while an itching right palm means he will give it away. These attributions are sometimes reversed, as the details vary according to who is listing them.

The person who tries *to palm off* something he doesn't want to someone else is an underhanded character. He resembles the prototypical cardsharp who, even as far back as the 1600s, stole a glance at the card he was about to deal himself, and which, if it didn't suit him, he hid in his palm. He continued the maneuver by dealing himself another card and finally passing that first, hidden card on to another player. Such deceit led to the creation of rules such as "all hands above the table," but expert cheaters still succeed with just their palms. An interesting but now obsolete term is "straight-fingered," which described the innocent person whose fingers could not even bend to hold anything obtained dishonestly.

FINGER The term *ladyfinger* refers to many diverse items. In 1820 John Keats alluded to a biscuit of this name in his satirical poem "The Cap and Bells": "Steep some lady's-fingers nice in Candy wine." Around 1850 the English also applied the word to the vegetable okra and to a special tapered glass of liquid, usually gin. Australians gave the term by 1890 to a short, thin banana. It was also given to grapes of an obviously interesting shape; to cakes; and to the foxglove flower, whose Latin name is *digitalis,* or "belonging to the little finger." Another plant, called *Anthyllis vulneraria,* or the kidney vetch, is sometimes given this nickname, as are other grasses. Although Americans are probably most familiar with the word as the name of a long, slender sponge cake, "ladyfinger" is also the term for a variety of potato, one species of lobster, one strain of apples, and, derisively, for both unproductive corn and a

*To **twist** someone around one's finger*

cowardly person, as exemplified by a fighter with too light a punch to do any harm.

To twist someone around one's finger is the physical equivalent of the word "manipulate," from the Latin *manus*, meaning hand. In 1469 the phrase "to bring a person about one's thumb" described the same deliberate use of techniques to gain control over another person.

The story behind wearing a ring on one's *wedding finger* to signify a love bond supposedly comes from a writer of the second century A.D., Aulus Gellius. He recounted the assertion of the Latin historian Appianus that a delicate nerve runs from the fourth finger of the left hand directly to the heart. Because this finger—the *digitus annularis*, or "gold finger"—was thought to be so closely connected to the heart, the Greeks and Romans considered it a link to life itself and dubbed it the "medical finger." They would use the medical finger to stir potions in the belief that this finger, endowed with powers similar to those of a divining rod, would warn the heart if the finger came into contact with a harmful substance. A superstition that still exists is that it is bad luck to rub lotion into the skin or to scratch an itch with anything other than the medical finger. In *Pantagruel* (1533) Rabelais recounted, "At last he put on her medical finger a pretty handsome gold ring." In his 1680 *Treaties of Spousals*, Henry Swinburne supported this belief in a love link of some kind by stating that anatomists had discovered not a nerve but a vein called the *vena amoris*, the "vein of love," indeed running from the left finger to the heart. As romantic as this phenomenon sounds, it has never been substantiated, and neither a specific nerve nor vein has been found to be the physical basis for this ageless custom.

Both the naïve innocent and the deliberate gossip may inadvertently *burn their fingers,* or come to harm when meddling in other people's business. The phrase clearly originated in times past when open fires were a necessity. A person trying to fan a fire or check the contents of a pot cooking over an open flame could carelessly burn himself—especially if the pot was not his own—as a reward for his interference. Eric Partridge quoted the saying "Never burn your fingers to snuff another man's candle," while Collins wrote in his *Proverbs,* "The busiebody burns his own fingers."

It is a well-known superstition *to keep one's fingers crossed* for good luck. People have for centuries made the sign of the cross on their bodies to ask for blessing, to affirm their faith, and to ward off evil spirits. Crossing one's fingers is simply the least obvious, most private way to ask for protection. The most common cross made with one's fingers is the St. Andrew's Cross, in which one places the second finger of the right hand on top of the first. The Greek Cross is made by placing the first finger of one hand on top of the knuckle of the first finger of the other hand, keeping the fingers at right angles. Though the fingers may be crossed for just a second, that should be time enough for the powers to do their work. Children sometimes try to worm their way out of being punished for lying by maintaining that a lie doesn't count if it was told while one's fingers were crossed. How to win that argument? It is necessary to use a ploy as clever as the oath often sworn in the 1700s and the 1800s, in which one bent one's elbow and intoned aloud that it should never become straight again if what was being stated was not the truth. However, this obsolete practice of "Crook my elbow and never get straight" was outdone by the even more persuasive gesture and accompanying oath of "Cross my heart and hope to die"—an effective display of bravado that might well have caused listeners, afraid of sudden changes in their own luck, to cross their own fingers, hastily and furtively.

Judging by *rule of thumb* means arriving at a general assessment based more on practical experience than on scientific methods. The repetition involved in measuring lengths of material led country merchants long ago to use something that was always on hand—namely, a part of their thumb—as a unit approximating one inch. In the 1700s business people kept their public relations smooth by apportioning one inch more than the requested amount to allow for possible error. Employing other body parts for measuring was also common practice, as is obvious with the adoption of "hand" to equal four inches and "foot" to equal twelve inches. Less well known is the cubit, a measurement of eighteen to twenty-one inches as determined by the length of the forearm from the elbow to the middle finger. The ell is a unit of length no longer in use probably because of the confusion it caused. Its distance varied from twenty-seven to forty-three inches, depending on whether one used the elbows or the legs to determine its measure, for at one time an ell was the length of one's arms from elbow to elbow, and at another time it was the length of the leg from the thigh to the knee—all this depending on which country one was in. More accurate is the fathom, which is equal to six feet and is based on the distance between the opposite fingertips of a man's outstretched arms. Another explanation of the expression originates from the brewery. Before the development of pasteurization, a brewer tested the temperature of his brew by putting his thumb into the beer mixture. Thomas Hardy gave the phrase broader application by having Michael Henchard, in *The Mayor of Casterbridge,* describe himself thus: "Unluckily, I am bad at figures—a rule of thumb sort of man." Besides measures, weights were also determined by thumb. In the 1600s a tiny container the depth of a thumb was said to hold a thumbful, or a small number, of grains.

The implications of the phrase *to be under one's thumb*—a parallel to the phrase *to twist someone around one's finger*—depend on whether one is utterly subservient to someone else, sometimes under his influence, or only occasionally at his disposal. In 1586 the writer John Hooker commented in his *History of Ireland* that "Diuerse other secret vnderminers, who wrought so cunninglie vnder the thumbe . . . their malice would not have been in manner suspected." In 1809 Benjamin Malkin translated the teasing observation made by Le Sage, the author of *Adventures of Gil Blas:* "Authors . . . are under the thumb of booksellers and players." The grievous consequence of being totally at the mercy of others is most apparent in the next phrase.

Thumbs down is a negative vote, whether or not actual thumbs come into play. *Verso pollice* was a Latin term for the signal that the ancient Romans used to condemn a defeated gladiator to death. There is conflict today as to which gesture the Romans actually employed, since *verso* only means "turned." Nor does a direction for "up" or "down" appear in the term *pollice primo,* the vote for mercy, which was indicated by concealing the thumb in the fist by tucking it under the closed fingers, as though sheathing a dagger. By the 1800s, however, the phrases "thumbs up" and "thumbs down" applied to support and disapproval in a more general way.

The expression *to be all thumbs,* or to be extremely clumsy, dates back to 1546, when John Heywood wrote in his *Proverbs,* "Whan he should get ought [out], eche fynger is a thumbe." By 1579 it had been recorded as a recognized idiom. The beauty of its versatility is seen in an 1870 quote from *Echo:* "Your uneducated man is all thumbs, as the phrase runs; and what education does for him is to supply him with clever fingers."

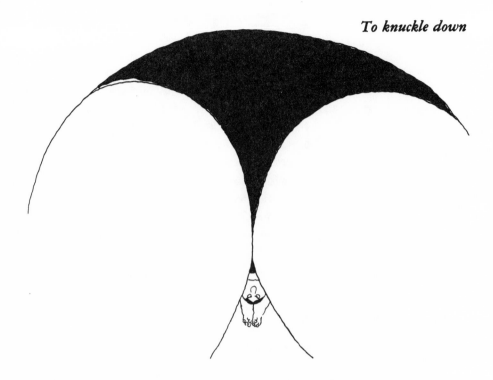

A person has *to knuckle down* to a difficult task by applying himself earnestly to it, as one does when putting one's *shoulder to the wheel* (see page 50). In a heated game of marbles in the 1700s—when the game was known as "playing taw"—players would advise each other to "knuckle down to your taw," or place the entire hand on the ground as close as possible to the marbles, and put one's weight on the knuckles for better leverage. Another possible derivation for the term is the fact that the bones of the spinal column were once called knuckles. By seriously knuckling down to work, a person both literally and figuratively puts his back into it.

An unbearable burden may cause a person *to knuckle under* or give in to strain, either physical or mental.

KNUCKLE

In the past the word "knuckle" pertained not only to the joints of the fingers and spinal column but also to the joints at the knee and elbow, especially to the round part of the bone that is exposed when the joint is bent. Today one can still find cuts of meat referred to as knuckles. The idea of yielding to a stronger force comes from medieval times, when a defeated leader would kneel before his conqueror, placing the knuckles of his knees on the ground in acknowledgment of his humbled position.

Knuckle-dusters are brass knuckles, the metal coverings intended both to shield the wearer's hand from injury and to add force to his punch. Ancient Roman gladiators wore the finger-guard called a *cestus,* decorated with engraved designs and enhanced by sharp projections of varying lengths. Unlike the Roman fashion, today's version offers the advantage that it can be pocketed. Since the 1800s the slip-on style with four-finger protection has remained fairly uniform. The instrument still elicits the response alluded to in an account in the July 1861 publication *All Year Round:* "But what the crew most feared, was the free use of the 'brass knuckles' or 'knuckle dusters' . . . they constitute a regular portion of the equipment of an officer of the American mercantile marine." In England "knuckle-duster" is a slang term used to refer to gaudy and ostentatious rings.

A rap on the knuckles is a sharp reproof, at one time referred to as "a hit over the thumbs" and at another, "crossing one over the thumbs." In 1548 Joseph Hall recounted in his *Chronicles of Henry VII* that "In the later ende of hys oracion, he a little rebuked the lady Margaret and hyt her on the thombes." The common image of a punitive teacher has been largely superseded by a more figurative interpretation of the phrase. Mary Kingsley confessed in her 1897 work, *Travels in West Africa,* that she received "a severe rap on my moral knuckles from my conscience."

The Torso

To make a clean breast of something is the equivalent of "to get something off one's chest," for both expressions stem from the medieval concept that the various organs and their secretions were responsible for different emotions. The heart, not the head, was considered the seat of one's thoughts and feelings, a romantic notion that hasn't been altogether rejected even today. Our forefathers interpreted the phrase literally and punished sinners by branding them with letters or symbols that identified the crimes they had committed. Hester Prynne, in Hawthorne's *The Scarlet Letter,* was sentenced to wear the letter "A" as a sign of adultery, and so in a very real sense could not get her guilt off her chest. She would have been grateful to follow Macbeth's advice to "Cleanse the stuff'd bosom of that perilous stuff which weighs upon the heart." As informed as people are today, many would still attest to a feeling of lightening within the chest upon unburdening their troubled minds.

BREAST

To keep abreast with, meaning to keep up-to-date, has its roots in military history. As far back as 1579 troops were drilled to march "with breasts or fronts in a line," as *The Oxford English Dictionary* puts it, in order to provide the best defense against oncoming attackers. A century later the phrase applied to ship

*Scratch my back and
I'll scratch yours*

formations, for, in 1679, strategy in naval battles
called for arranging several lines of ships abreast of
each other, as again *The Oxford English Dictionary*
states, "with ships equally distant and parallel." The
phrase was quickly adopted after the mid-1600s to
mean keeping current with things, especially being
prepared to meet them head-on if necessary.

BACK *Scratch my back and I'll scratch yours* is a euphemism
for exchanging favors to each party's satisfaction.
Very much a vernacular expression, the phrase ap-

plies more to coarse business dealings than to sophisticated legal agreements. Since the Middle Ages, when the word "claw" was used in place of "scratch," the phrase has carried suggestions of manipulation and flattery to gain influence in higher places.

A monkey on one's back is a burden that hangs on and refuses to let go, such as a drug addict's dependence on both drugs and their pushers. His physical need causes him financial strain, while the insistent pusher adds more weight for the addict's back to bear. The phrase is undoubtedly a relative of "a turkey on one's back," a common nineteenth-century expression synonymous with "drunk."

A pig would not be an easy item *to carry piggyback.* Actually, the pig entered the phrase erroneously, the result of repeated mispronunciation of the original "pick-a-back" or "pack-a-back," a reference to the method of carrying a bundle on one's shoulders or back as cited in literature since the 1500s. The phrase passed through many mutations, such as "pick back," "pick pack," and "pig-a-back" before settling into its current form over a hundred years ago.

The frequently overlooked origin of the square-dance step called the *do-si-do* lies in an anglicization of the French *dos-à-dos,* which means simply "back to back." Participants in the dance, their arms folded across their chests, circle their partners to the left or right, each at one point having his back to the other. The term was also the name of a French carriage in which people sat back to back.

RIB The words *spare-ribs,* meaning the cut of meat consisting of closely trimmed ribs with the shoulder removed, are an example of the transposition of terms through popular use. The Middle-Late German *ribbesper* became "ribspare" and, later, "spear-rib." As early as 1596 Thomas Nashe in *Have With You to Saffron Walden* poked fun at a contemporary in writing, "Let's have half a dozen spare ribs of his rethorique, with tart sauce of taunts correspondent." Users of the term were obviously aware of its confusing forms, for in 1736 a writer named Samuel Pegge recorded in *Kenticisms,* "So, in Kent, to 'wrong-take' a person is to take him wrong . . . and a 'ribspare' is a spare rib." Both of these quotes carry the same joshing tone as the related phrase "to rib a person," which clearly came from the relentless teaser who poked his victim in the ribs.

Eat your heart out has lost the romantic, sympathetic overtones that Edmund Spenser intended to convey when in 1596 he wrote in *The Faerie Queene,* "He could not rest; but did his stout heart eat." John Lyly had already cautioned in 1579 "not to eat out heartes," that is, to suffer so from continuous grief and longing as to consume in a figurative sense the organ directing one's passions, which was formerly believed to be the heart and not the mind. Nowadays the phrase is flung in acid tones to put a jealous person in his place, without much thought given to the extent of his grief. HEART

To have one's heart in the right place has its roots in the Middle Ages too, when people believed not only that the heart (as opposed to the mind) controlled a person's emotions, but also that the heart could move up and down from its home in the upper chest. Many expressions arose from this fanciful theory. *To have one's heart in one's mouth* means to become alarmed as a result of having the heart jump and momentarily choke the subject. A 1430 hymn

His heart sank into his boots

expressed the physical sensation of spirits sinking with the words, "Myn herte fil doun vnto my too [toe]." In the mid-1500s, John Heywood wrote in *Proverbs,* "Your heart is in your hose all in dispaire." Seventeenth-century quotations place the heart in one's heels and then in one's shoes. By the eighteenth century the quintessential expression for dejection and fear emerged as *his heart sank into his boots.* Correspondingly, the Latin phrase *Cor illi in genua decidet*—literally, *his heart sinks to his knees*—means that fear makes the knees shake. With all this roaming around of body parts, it is no surprise that the contemporary reference to the person whose heart is in the right place describes one who remains constant and whose mind, successor to the heart as the seat of emotion, is responsible for his fine character.

A person *learns by heart* in committing something to memory. A throwback to at least the fourteenth century and probably earlier, the phrase again refers to the belief that the heart was the controlling center of a person's emotions, intelligence, and even memory. The French verb *se recorder,* which has the same meaning, comes from the Latin word *cor,* or heart, as does the English word "record."

The expression *to warm the cockles of one's heart,* or to cause pleasure or sympathetic feelings, originated with the sleuthing of anatomists in the seventeenth century, when people still held that the heart ruled the emotions. Anatomists compared the valves of a shellfish, the ribbed, heartshaped cockleshell, called *conchyllium* in Latin, to the ventricles, or *cochleae cordis,* within a human heart. By metaphorical extension, as deeply contained inside the heart as were the ventricles or cockles, so deeply held also were the emotions of a person. Warming the cockles has remained a common way of expressing how intensely one is affected by pleasure, but the image of the shellfish associated with the phrase has often been overlooked.

Nowadays the individual who *wears his heart on his sleeve*—as Iago promised to do in *Othello*—exposes his motives and affections with less certainty of reciprocation than did knights in medieval times. It was the custom then for a knight to tie a ribbon, scarf, or some other memento belonging to his lady to his sleeve, openly declaring whom he was going to fight for. As time did not honor the custom, today the phrase refers to a person who shows his feelings too readily to provide the suspense vital to many relationships.

Why does the phrase *hearts and flowers* mean sentimentality itself? These two symbols of romance were innocently joined in the title of a song popular around 1910, the tune of which perfectly captured that yearning, bittersweet quality guaranteed to evoke a sympathetic response from listeners. Overkill, perhaps by violinists who played the tune too often as background music to a tearful scene, must have done the phrase in. The song title passed from the specific to the generic, so that even people who had never heard the piece responded to sentimental situations by playing imaginary violins.

As antiquated as it may sound, the term *lily-livered,* or *white-livered,* is very much alive. An editorial in the July 21, 1979, issue of *Saturday Review* announced: "We have had enough of partisan Presidents—whether they see the enemy as Commie-kids . . . or oil barons and lily-livered Congresspersons." The expression, a synonym for "yellow-bellied," stems from the fourteenth century, when the liver, like other internal organs at one time or another, was thought to be responsible for passion. The belief was that the darker the bile produced by the liver, the stronger the passion of its owner. A light or white-colored liver having little bile meant that the owner lacked spirit and courage, or, in today's slang, no "guts." Shakespeare apparently subscribed to this physiological linking of the liver and the flushed face with bravery, for in *Henry V* he described his character thus: "For Bardolph, he is white-livered and red-faced; by the means whereof, 'a faces it out, but fights not." Furthermore, in *Macbeth* he assailed cowardliness by writing, "Go prick thy face and over-red thy fear, thou lily-livered boy."

LIVER

GALL
BLADDER

On a literal level, *You have a lot of gall* simply means that your gall bladder is storing too much of the bile secreted by the liver, thus preventing the bile from reaching the intestine, where it helps to digest your food. A sour, greenish fluid, the dark bile that medieval anatomists admired as being indicative of strong passion led to the formation of this expression meaning bitter feeling that amounts almost to rude boldness. More than "cheek" or "nerve," having too much gall implies that one's outright insolence is the result of accumulated rancorous feelings, blocked and boiling within the bile- or gall-producing organ. Although during the Middle Ages people were perceptive enough to recognize the relationship between the flow of body fluids and health, their methods of inducing the fluids to release harmful elements seldom resulted in the balance they tried to attain (see *sense of humor*, pages 119–21).

STOMACH

To turn one's stomach, now a cliché for disgust, has appeared in the writings of such writers as Alexander Pope, who wrote in 1738, "This filthy simile ... Quite turns my stomach." People living in the Middle Ages attributed many traits and duties to the stomach: at one time or another, the noun "stomach" represented not only digestion itself but also spirit, pride, resentment, and even one's total disposition.

Anger or frustration might cause a person *to vent his* SPLEEN
spleen, or to release all his emotions in a fit of bad
temper. The Polish have a phrase for it: *wylac swa
zolcic* means "to have a yellow quarrel." The mysteri-
ous spleen, which scientific research has found is
responsible for regulating the components of blood,
was thought during the Middle Ages to be involved
somehow with temperament. From around 1300 to
1600, many believed that it produced laughter. Conversely, in the 1500s the spleen was also blamed for
low spirits, melancholy feelings, spite, malice, and
erratic bursts of wild behavior—in other words, for
excitability and bad temper. Blood-letting to "get
out the bad blood" believed to be concentrated in
one area was a common remedy for a person's
changeable moods. Although such literal spleen-
venting proved unwise, the idea of finding relief
through emotional release remained.

A man of my kidney and *of the same kidney* are both KIDNEY
expressions as old as the late Middle Ages and are
remarkable for having been used that long ago to
describe two people of similar temperament. As
were other organs, the kidney was considered at
that time by many to be the seat of affection. Only

today do we know the importance of typing kidneys for compatibility in transplants, so that it is momentarily humbling to find sixteenth-century philosophers and playwrights explaining the rapport between individuals as Shakespeare did in *The Merry Wives of Windsor*: "Think of that, a man of my kidney, think of that, that am as subject to heate as butter."

APPENDIX   In the same way that the *appendix* is the outgrowth of the large intestine and not vital to its proper functioning, the appendix of a book is a supplement containing material relevant to the work but not essential for it to be complete. Appropriately, the word comes from the Latin *pendere,* to hang or suspend. As far back as 1549, a certain Hugh Latimer wrote in his *Sermon before Edward VI* of having assembled "The commentaries, contayning the solemnities of their religion wyth manye other appendixes."

LOINS   The advice *Gird up your loins* suggests preparing oneself for great exertion or protecting oneself from an attack. In Biblical times men braced themselves for action by lifting their loose-fitting leg coverings and actually tying them around—or girding—their loins, the section of the body between the ribs and hips. By wrapping their garments around the body, the men could move more easily in a fight, or when traveling or doing difficult physical work. The Book of Luke urges preparation for the coming of the Messiah: "Let your loins be girded about." In 1667 John Milton included the expression in *Paradise Lost* in which he wrote, "Some Tree whose broad smooth Leaves together sowd, And girded on our loyns, may cover round Those middle parts." Implicit in the expression is the understanding that binding the bottom half of the torso ensures the protection of the area most vital to regeneration and strength—the genitals. In his 1697 translation of *The Works of Virgil,* John Dryden wrote, "What boots it [is] that from Phoebus' loins I spring." Literary uses since then have extended the scope of the expression beyond the physical to include the notion of gathering up one's wits and summoning up one's inner strength to meet a challenge.

BOWELS

Bowels of compassion is another phrase that owes its existence to the medieval belief that organs and their secretions were the sources of emotions. In the 1500s bowels were thought to be responsible for one's capacity for sympathy and pity. At different times the word "bowels" meant the interior of the body, then any large interior, the large intestine itself, the organ that passes waste from the intestine, and, finally, an abbreviated term for the waste matter itself. *The Oxford English Dictionary* cites many qualities figuratively associated with bowels, including pity, humanity, tenderness, mercy, and one mentioned in this advice from 1526: "Close not your bowells of charite from them."

From Leg to Toe

Break a leg! seems a strange way to wish someone
good luck. Although it became popular as a theater
idiom, its origins may reach back into European
folklore. Some common superstitions claim that
saying the opposite of what one wishes is actually
the best way of getting what one really wants. Carrying an umbrella to ensure that it won't rain is in
the same spirit as wishing a skier *Hals-und-Beinbruch!,* an old German expression for "May you
break your neck and leg." "Hals-und-Beinbruch!"
also became a slogan of reassurance for actors in the
German and Yiddish theater of the early twentieth
century. In English it became—with the neck
omitted—a wish for luck in general. In the Italian
theater, actors tap the head of a wolfhound or similar dog for luck before a performance while uttering
an idiom meaning "into the mouth of the wolf," an
equivalent of "break a leg." Theatrical folklore explains the phrase by asserting that a healthy actor
would do well to emulate the success of the otherwise less fortunate Sarah Bernhardt, even though
she had one leg amputated late in life. In the late
1600s the phrase was used in a very different context
that implied a more negative connotation: a
woman of the lower classes was said to have "broken a leg" when she delivered an illegitimate child.

A game leg is a variation on "a lame leg," meaning a leg that is defective. Its origin is not altogether certain, although Grose's slang dictionary of the late 1700s defined the dialect word "gam" as a derivative of the Welsh *cam,* meaning crooked or unsure. Joseph Wright's *English Dialect Dictionary* of the late nineteenth century, a more respected authority, substantiated this definition by terming "game" a colloquial word for lame or crooked. Other sources cite an early dialect term "gammy," related both to the Old French *gambi,* meaning bent or crooked, and to the modern French word for leg, *jambe.*

To pull one's leg, or to delude or poke fun at someone, is mentioned in an 1867 Scottish rhyme about cheating:

> He preached an' at last drew the auld body's leg
> Sae the kirk got the gatherins o' our Aunty Meg.

The conniving preacher "drew" or "pulled" Meg's leg, persuading her to leave her money to his church rather than to her family. Pulling the leg is associated with trickery simply because an aggressor aims to embarrass his victim by literally or figuratively tripping him, leaving him with "only one leg to stand on."

Bandy-legged, or bow-legged, is a seventeenth-century term incorporating an object unfamiliar to most people today. A curved stick called a "bandy" was the main piece of equipment used in "bandy-ball," a game similar to hockey. The bowed shape easily lent itself to describing legs having that tendency. In 1849 Washington Irving graphically described one of his characters as being "Short and bandy-legged . . . his little legs curving like a pair of parentheses below his kilt."

The *knee-jerk response* (the patellar reflex in medical KNEE terminology) was coined by a certain Dr. Gowers in the mid-1800s. This well-known phenomenon, the automatic kicking response of the leg when the tendon below the patella, or kneecap, is struck, was once called the "knee-jump." It sprang out of medical dictionaries and into current jargon to describe a slavish act done without thinking.

As American as *shindig* sounds, its origins go back SHIN to another seventeenth-century British ball game. "Shindy," "shinny," and "shinty" were all names for a game similar to field hockey during which the coach or observers might have shouted either "Shin ye!"—a warning for the players to protect themselves—or *Sinteag!*—a Gaelic word for "jump" or "skip." By the 1800s shindig meant both a party and the particular dance sailors performed by jumping and kicking their heels up in the air to the side, level with their knees. The term is currently popular in the southern United States, but the idea that it earned its name from a sharp blow to the shins received at a merry party down South where people kicked up their heels is highly doubtful.

FOOT AND FEET

The person left *to foot the bill* assumes the responsibility of paying for an expense. In 1623 a certain Bishop Andrewes explained the phrase simply enough in his *Sermons:* "So, it signifies to make the foot of an account. We call it the foot, because we write it below at the foot." Since that time the phrase has transcended its literal interpretation. Today it often refers to having to account for transactions in which money may or may not be an issue and which often involve more than just the payment of a bill.

Having *one foot in the grave* describes someone who is a mere footstep away from his demise. The fourth-century Roman emperor Julian did not fear death's approach, for he vowed to "learn something even if he had one foot in the grave." Greek mythology made reference to having "one foot in Charon's ferryboat," an allusion to the voyage after death across the river Styx to the blissful Elysian Fields.

To have an itching foot is the last entry in a long succession of popular superstitions that attach significance to itching. As previously discussed, the person with itching ears supposedly enjoys hearing gossip and the one with itchy palms eagerly invites

One foot in the grave

bribes. An itchy nose means that the sufferer will have a fight, kiss a fool, or give other people reason to gossip about him. If someone's upper lip itches, he will be kissed by a tall person; if his lower lip itches, he will be kissed by a short person. When both lips itch, he wants to repeat gossip. Finally, the itching foot indicates an urge to travel. A very superstitious person planning a trip should avoid both leaving on a Friday and carrying a black suitcase. He should also be sure to lead with his right foot when he leaves home, for using the left would cause him to go where he would not be welcome.

The advice to *put one's best foot forward,* or to make enormous efforts to present oneself to one's best advantage, has a history rich in literal interpretations of the phrase. A very early superstition maintained that the right foot, as the natural counterpart of the right hand, was the "best foot." The ancient Romans so feared the unlucky associations of "left" (see *left-handed compliment,* pages 55–57) that, according to Petronius and Augustus, a person—literally the first "footman"—was stationed at the front door of one's house to insist that visitors entered right foot first. Leaving any room with the left foot forward was also taking a chance, just as leaving home for a trip with the left foot first guaranteed rejection all along the route. Pythagoras taught that one should put one's right shoe on before the left. In addition, during the warming-up exercises that Romans called "getting their feet in" for a race, they made sure to position themselves at the starting line with right foot in front. By Shakespeare's time the phrase had assumed a more figurative meaning, for the advice in *King John* reads: "Nay, but make haste; the better foot before." Today when someone says, "I hope he got off on the right foot," he seldom realizes how literally the phrase was once meant to be interpreted. Another bit of foot folklore—this one maintaining that *both* feet were "best"—claimed that a child born feet first would have magical healing powers in later life. A further superstition persists in remote areas of northern England and Scotland, where in the early hours of New Year's Day people still perform the ceremony of welcoming the "First Foot" into one's house. The first visitor on January 1 is meant to guarantee a good year by bringing gifts of bread, coal, salt, coins, and evergreen branches symbolizing food, warmth, wealth, health, and continuing life. It is important that the First Foot be a man (a woman is considered unlucky) and that he not have flat feet, crossed eyes, red hair, or eyebrows that meet above the nose. In order to ensure that the year starts off right, village folk deliberately seek out a suitable dark-haired stranger epitomizing the mystery of the new year, assign him the role of First Foot, and provide him, just before midnight, with the proper gifts to bring early the next day. Choosing an appropriate First Foot means literally putting the best foot forward into one's house.

The person who *puts his foot into something* commits the mistake the French refer to as a *faux pas*, or a false step. He gets himself into as deep a mess as the proverbial bishop who appeared in the colorful seventeenth- and eighteenth-century saying, "The bishop hath put his foot in." In those times, whenever someone burned the milk or meat he was cooking, he excused himself by invoking the bishop described in the *1811 Dictionary of the Vulgar Tongue* as a scapegoat: "Formerly, when a bishop passed through a village, all the inhabitants ran out of their houses to solicit his blessing, even leaving their milk, etc. on the fire, to take its chance, which, when burnt, was said to be bishoped."

The shoe is on the other foot expresses the smug satisfaction felt when, as a result of circumstances finally reversing themselves, an enemy experiences the suffering he once inflicted on his victims. He endures pain equal to the discomfort of wearing his left shoe on his right foot. The Bible contains many references that recognize the significance of feet, not the least of which is the washing of a guest's feet as a sign of hospitality. There is also the ancient Hebrew ceremony called *halitzah* that involves the taking off of the shoe to announce the breaking of a contract, as illustrated in the Book of Ruth. A widow who, like Ruth, had no sons was saved from becoming someone else's dependent by the Hebrew law of *yibbum*, which declared that if a man died without heirs, his brother or nearest relative, even if already married, was duty-bound to marry the widow. In Ruth's case the nearest kinsman fortunately declined, freeing her to marry Boaz. To make that refusal valid, the same male relative had to perform in a court of law the *halitzah* rite dictated in Deuteronomy. He put on a shoe reserved specifically for that ceremony. The widow then removed the shoe, symbolically breaking the contract, and spat in front of him. While in Ruth's situation all parties were satisfied, a man's open refusal to marry his brother's widow was not generally encouraged. By publicly rejecting her, he risked his own reputation, for it usually followed that he would in turn be rejected, and thus in a sense would experience the pain of wearing a shoe on the other foot.

The expression *to be on a good footing with someone* is synonymous with saying that two people share a friendly understanding. The phrase is actually based on an old French expression, *Etre sur un grand pied dans le monde,* that translates loosely as "He has a large foot in society." The "large foot" is a reference not only to Henry VIII's *grand pied,* but also to the supposition during his time that a person's rank was determined by the size of his foot. Ergo Henry's easy justification for his superior position, which was arrived at by as convenient a method of determining whom to associate with as the Greek differentiation of "patrician" versus "plebeian" according to the length of one's middle toes. By the eighteenth century, "footing" came to mean the metaphorical measure of one person's relationship with another. It is startling to realize that one of our figurative expressions for describing personal relationships originated from the calculation of how many inches a man's foot extended.

It is always unsettling to discover that a person has *feet of clay,* or a flaw that previously went undetected in what seemed to be an exemplary character. The Biblical Daniel interpreted a dream for King Nebuchadnezzar in which a figure having a head of gold, arms and breast of silver, belly and thighs of brass, legs of iron, and feet of part iron and part clay broke apart and floated away in the wind when a stone struck the feet—the weakest part of the statue. Daniel's explanation to the king followed the same line of thought as the proverbial lesson involving the weakest link in a chain. Even a well-disguised, small defect in one's character can become the cause of a person's—or a kingdom's—complete downfall.

The expression *to get cold feet* has both a physiological and literary background. Today we know that fear slows down the circulation of blood to the extremities, causing them to feel cold and move less easily. Back in the sixteenth and seventeenth centuries, cardplayers in Lombardy, Italy, unaware of the relationship between fear and blood circulation, popularized the saying *Avegh minga frecc i pee,* loosely meaning that their feet got cold when they were losing money and wanted to quit the game. Moneylenders also used the expression to state that their funds were low. Ben Jonson incorporated the phrase in his 1605 play, *Volpone,* in which his main character explains why he situated his bank not in the center of Venice but in a more remote corner of the Piazza San Marco: "Let me tell you: I am not, as your Lombard proverb saith, cold on my feet; or content to part with my commodities at a cheaper rate than I am accustomed; look not for it." Confident of his cash supply, Volpone was not eager to strike any bargains. Today a person with metaphorical cold feet withdraws from a situation because fear makes him reluctant to move ahead.

Nowadays the expression *to sit or lie at a person's feet* implies a loyal, almost servile attitude, but in ancient times it meant a daring, heartfelt gesture. When, in the Book of Ruth, Boaz awoke to find Ruth lying at his feet, he understood that in accordance with custom she was willingly offering herself to him, the one whom she believed to be the nearest kinsman of her dead husband. Her further act of "uncovering his feet"—a Biblical euphemism for removing his robe—was additional proof of the sincerity of her choice and her pledge of loyalty. Through overuse the phrase developed strongly derogatory overtones, similar to those acquired by *kowtow* (see page 6).

Why include the expression *to mind your p's and q's* in a section about feet? Although there are many legends to explain it, a popular story holds that the phrase comes from the seventeenth and eighteenth centuries, when the influence of King Louis XIV was very strong. This era of lavish decoration, elaborate fashions, fussy hairstyles, and exaggerated gestures set a premium on good manners and other social graces. Imagine the ensuing embarrassment if one didn't watch out for one's "p's," or *pieds,* for "feet," and "q's," or *queues,* for "wigs," when dancing or making a low bow.

HEEL   One of the most common expressions containing a body part is *Achilles heel.* It is ironic that the attempt in Greek mythology by Thetis, the mother of Achilles, to make her son invulnerable by immersing him in the river Styx resulted in his undoing. The only unprotected area of his body was the spot on his tendon where she grasped him and held him upside down, and it was there that Achilles was struck by the fatal arrow shot by Paris and directed by Apollo in the final stages of the Trojan War. The Achilles heel has become a well-known symbol for the weakest part of any situation. In an 1810 article for the weekly paper *The Friend,* Samuel Coleridge described Ireland as "that vulnerable heel of the British Achilles." In his 1864 work, *Frederick the Great,* Carlyle referred to the unprotected state of "Hanover ... the Achilles'-heel to invulnerable England."

Being forced *to cool one's heels,* or to wait and calm down, is an expression as old as man's first attempts at transportation. A long journey not only tires the legs of a horse but also causes its hoofs to become overheated, so that the single rider or driver of a horse-drawn vehicle had to stop frequently and wait for the hoofs to cool off. He undoubtedly dealt with the impatience of his passengers at having their schedules delayed by telling them to cool their heels also. In this connection it is amusing to note that the expression "hold your horses" shares the same meaning and very possibly the same derivation. The Dutch have a colorful phrase to describe this imposition on one's time and one's resulting irritation, namely *staan blaubekken,* which literally means "standing in the cold until one's lips turn blue."

The common expression *down at the heels,* coined around 1500 in a form similar to "out at the heels," applied originally not just to shoes but to any worn-out foot covering. To be slipshod is literally to be slipping out of one's shoes, walking with one's heels squashing the backs of the shoes. A closely related phrase is "on one's uppers," or having heels so worn down that the wearer seems to be walking on the soles alone. By the 1700s the current phrase took hold as a figurative description of a person whose life is in as sorry a state as his eroded shoes.

In contrast with the previous expression, *to be well-heeled* obviously means that one has enough money to be not only elegantly shod but also well-off in general. The idea that money can provide the solution to problems was not the original intent of the expression, which first applied to outfitting game cocks for a fight. Cock-fighting was an eighteenth-century American pastime in which, like boxing, spectators bet on which of the two combatants would defeat the other. To gain an advantage, owners resorted to attaching artificial spurs to their roosters' feet before the fight. The same need to feel secure in unexpected situations led people to carry weapons in their boots in anticipation of trouble. A

Well-heeled

person felt reassured at being sufficiently armed or "heeled" to be able to defend himself. Such inner confidence was especially important during the Civil War and the settling of the West, when the expression gained in popularity. It was then only a short step to the contemporary concept of money as a weapon that automatically gives one security.

TOE

To toe the mark implies meeting a previously set standard of performance. The phrase comes from the early days of prizefighting when both parties had to be literally "up to scratch" during an entire match. In the days before strict rules were established, a fight consisted more of butchery than skill. To protect fighters from being badly beaten and possibly even dying, a rule was imposed that the fight could not continue unless each contestant could stand up unassisted and scratch a designated mark with his toes, thereby proving that he was capable of continuing—hence the origin of the popular phrase "up to scratch." From the 1800s on, the phrase came to mean conforming to defined rules, whether they be the actual rules of running races—in which a contestant places the toes of one foot into position on the starting line upon hearing the signal "on your mark" and then advances "on his toes" into the race—or the rules of accepted behavior beyond the world of sports. In his *Two Years Before the Mast*, Richard Dana wrote, "The chief mate . . . marked a line on the deck, brought the two boys up to it, making them 'toe the mark.' "

Holding It All Together

Body English, a language of movement without words, is the result of a player's natural wish to guide the ball he has hit in a certain direction. Originating in the early 1900s, the phrase first applied to a particular spin on billiard balls and baseballs. Further differentiation gave birth to the term "bottom-English" for the combination of back- and sidespin. The "English" of the expression is not geographical. It merely recognizes the limits of communicating only with words. When gaps in spoken language occur, the language of gestures can complete the thought. The body expresses its need to direct the ball by instinctively contorting itself into the line of play it wants the ball to take—a line which, more often than not, fails to coincide with the path the ball actually follows. How much more literal a "follow-through" could there be?

Problems during any period in history have made it difficult *to keep body and soul together.* But the phrase actually stems from superstitions that arose during the Middle Ages and perhaps even earlier. People believed that a person's soul could easily escape from his body when he sneezed, leaving the body wide open to the devil. Such a fear led to saying "God bless you" for reassurance, since it followed that if a sneeze could suddenly force a person's soul out through his nostrils, then immediate action was crucial to prevent the devil from blocking the soul's return to the body. As faith was the answer to most needs, a friend's quick response of "God bless you" would suffice both to keep the devil away and to unite body and soul once more. Our phrase "beside oneself" is an obvious relative: emotional stress can change a person's behavior so markedly that it is as though his soul has left his body and is standing next to him, waiting for the right conditions to return and make him whole again.

SKIN *To skin the cat* means to execute a gymnastic maneuver in which a gymnast grasps a horizontal bar, raises his legs and feet up between his arms, and draws his body up over the bar either backward or forward. The name probably comes from observing cats' expertise at sinuously sneaking through openings narrow enough to graze the skin under their fur. But looking beyond the physical level, one sees that the phrase takes in not only the agility of cats but also their elusiveness, their ability to escape just when they are about to be cornered. Mark Twain used the phrase in the late 1800s to describe persons trying to evade issues, and an article in a *New York Evening Post* of 1905 stated, "We have learned how to hide behind the back log of 'environment' or to 'skin the cat' in morality on the score of 'heredity.' "

Persons who engage in *a skin game* find insidious ways to swindle money from their victims. Card-players from the 1800s literally "fleeced" each other in the appropriately named French game *lansquenet,* or "skin the lamb," in which players bet on which cards would win or lose as the dealer peeled away the cards, like layers of skin, from the deck. Around 1935 "skin game" became a derogatory term that critics applied to facial plastic surgery undergone by would-be glamorous women. Though unfair, the pun on "skin"—which suggested that one's money was being peeled away at the same time as one's flesh—was completely intentional.

The *galligaskins* one pictures as loosely fitting leggings were actually trousers worn during the sixteenth and seventeenth centuries. Although these pantaloons were worn next to the skin, the "skin" part of the word is the accidental result of the adoption of the original descriptive French term for these pants by the English and their alteration of the name to suit themselves. What was in French called *garguesque,* originating from the Italian *grechesca,* or Grecian, precisely because the garment was deliberately styled like the Greek undergarments of old, gained a new name in English and shed its etymological background.

The relatively new expression *slip me some skin* is a variation of "slap me five," an invitation to shake or slap hands in a gesture of friendship, the "five" referring to the five fingers of one person's hand that come into contact with those of another. A jive expression popular since the 1930s, its body language suggests one person extending his hand palm up for the other person to brush his own hand across, thus creating both a mild slap and a momentary bond between people.

SKELETON The presence, literal or figurative, of *a skeleton in the closet* is a constant source of embarrassment or pain that one tries in vain to conceal. Plutarch told the story of a custom the ancient Egyptians introduced to keep people from going out of control at celebrations at which pleasure often was the only goal. A skeleton intruded into the festivities as a reminder of the ever-present serious side of life. In his *Dictionary of Phrase and Fable,* E. Cobham Brewer explained how the skeleton made its way into the closet. Legend told of a long search to find even one person in the entire world with nothing to feel ashamed of, nothing hidden in his or her character or past. Only one woman seemed to pass the qualifications, but upon further scrutiny she also was found lacking. Investigators searching her home discovered a closet containing a human skeleton, the existence of which she attempted to rationalize by claiming, "I try to keep my trouble to myself, but every night my husband compels me to kiss that skeleton"—that skeleton being her former lover, whom her husband had killed in a duel. The use of a skeleton to symbolize a shameful secret is quite old, but it was only fairly recently recorded by William Thackeray in his 1845 *Punch in the East:* "There is a skeleton in every house."

Most students would probably define the expression *to bone up* for an exam as studying hard enough to make sure that the material becomes part of their inner workings—like their bones. As sound as this appears, the originator of the phrase is the Bohn Publishing Company, which published its own Classical Library books between 1860 and 1910. These translations of Greek and Latin works enabled students to "Bohn up" on their homework with the help of what we today call a "pony" or "trot" because, being a word-by-word translation, it keeps a steady pace with the original.

BONE

The expression *to have a bone to pick* originated in the sixteenth century, although throughout history people must have been familiar with the scrupulous time and attention a dog devotes to gnawing a bone. Having an unpleasant matter to settle can occupy a person's mind in a similar fashion. An unresolved bit of business could also be termed *a bone of contention,* or an issue likely to cause as much conflict as two dogs fighting over one bone. In the mid-1500s the author John Heywood wrote in his *Proverbs* that "The diuell [devil] hath cast a bone to

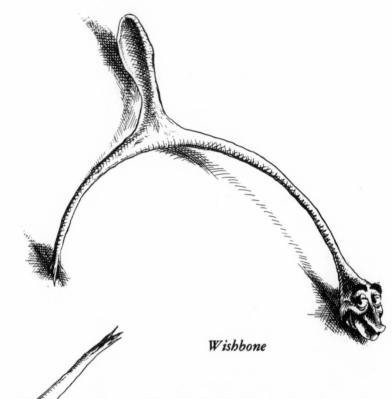

Wishbone

set stryfe betweene you." A letter to a curate in 1711 criticized church ritual: "The Liturgie, since it was first hatched, has been the bone of contention in England."

To hit the funny bone is the idiomatic equivalent of "to strike one's fancy" in a deliberately humorous manner. As any medical student knows, this nickname for the ulna, the bone of the upper arm that extends from the shoulder to the elbow, is a pun on its Latin name, *humerus*. The tingling that results from literally striking the funny bone is due to hitting the ulnar nerve—and that's not humorous at all.

Though technically not a human body part, the bone in the phrase *to make a wish on a wishbone* has an interesting past. A fowl's fork-shaped breastbone, called *furcula* in Latin, has been the source of a wishing game for two players since Shakespeare's time, when the game was poetically called "merry-thought." The belief then was that the winner—the one who broke off the longer side of the bone—would either get his wish or marry sooner than the other. The whimsical name "merrythought" did not survive, and that's a loss, for Americans have been acquainted with only the term "wishbone" since the mid-1800s.

The literal basis of *to make no bones about something* has hardly been called into question since the invention of modern food-straining devices. Around 1500, however, little bones posed a constant threat to those who swallowed their soup with total abandon; logically, no bones in the soup meant that the soup was no problem. As early as the sixteenth century, the phrase was already being used figuratively to indicate that no obstacles stood in a person's way. The current meaning that a person has no hesitation or objection was the message a writer named Joshua Sylvester intended back in his 1598 translation of *Divine Weeks and Works* of Guillaume du Bartas, in which he stated, "Hee . . . makes no bone to swear by God (for, hee beleeves there's none)."

JOINT   Why use the word *joint* for a marijuana cigarette? The place where muscles articulate, or meet, is the joint; the place where people meet, articulate or not, is wherever they may freely join together. Since the early 1800s "joint" has been an American slang term for any meeting place, and it was undoubtedly in such a small, secretive joint that marijuana was first shared socially. As a slang term for the cigarette, the word "joint" became popular in the 1950s.

Out of joint has special meaning for anyone who has suffered a dislocated bone. Comfort is not restored until the bone returns to its proper location. Similarly, people become disoriented when the rhythm of their daily lives is upset. The concept of harmony of the spheres and within the parts of the body was at the foundation of medieval man's relationship to his world. Although Shakespeare's *Hamlet* is the best-known source for early use of the phrase "The time is out of joint: O cursed spite that ever I was born to set it right," the lesser-known poet Thomas Hoccleve used it to describe mental and moral disarray in his directive *To Sir J. Oldcastle* (1415): "Thow haast been out of ioynt al to longe." It was also used by Sir Thomas More in his *Grafton Chronicles* (1513), in which he wrote, "They might peradventure bring the matter so farre out of ioynt, that it should never be brought in frame againe."

To breed bad blood, or to create dissension between **BLOOD** people, returns to the medieval concept which held that body organs and the balance of body fluids were responsible for a person's feelings and behavior. Blood was believed to be the seat of the emotions, particularly anger, and the temperature of the blood supposedly dictated one's temperament. If a person displayed a fit of anger, he needed to rid himself of the too hot "bad blood" causing the change in his personality. Consequently, bloodletting was a frequent recourse taken to eliminate the poisonous elements and thereby calm a person before he caused ill feelings, physical or mental, in other people. By the time bloodletting passed out of use as a cure-all, the phrase had acquired its more figurative connotation. In 1711 Jonathan Swift used the expression metaphorically in saying, "Hot words passed . . . and ill blood was plentifully bred."

If hot blood could get a person into trouble, one would presume that acts committed *in cold blood,* or those done rationally, not in the heat of passion, would be laudable. Taking the time to calculate one's moves means that one is clear-headed and in control of one's actions. All the more chilling, therefore, are the crimes committed in cold blood when one is able to deliberate every detail callously in advance. The French *sang froid* is an equivalent phrase. Although the medieval belief that blood temperature specifically controlled temperament has long been disproved (see previous entry), the increased blood circulation, pounding heartbeat, cold sweat, rush of adrenaline, and other body changes associated with the "fight or flight" syndrome, as well as the indignation one experiences when wrongly accused—all this still happens to everyone and gives credence to such phrases as "It made my blood run cold" and "It made my blood boil." In 1711 Joseph Addison reported in the *Spectator,* "It . . . looks like killing in cold blood," while in 1757 Tobias Smollett claimed in *The Reprisal,* that "We Englishmen never cut throats in cold blood."

Sweater

Seldom do we consider how an item as ordinary as a **SWEAT**
sweater earned its name. In the 1800s the sweater
was a particular garment designed to induce profuse
sweating. In different styles it was worn by a horse
or man undergoing exercises specifically to lose
weight. An article in the English publication *Sporting Magazine* in 1828 described "a craving, strong
horse, going along in his sweat, loaded with sweaters." Today's sweatsuits and sweaters work on the
principle of retaining body warmth, thereby keeping the body from catching cold.

The *sense of humor* that colors a person's outlook **HUMOR**
on life has its roots in a philosophy involving
body parts that dates back to the fourth century
B.C., when Hippocrates conceived his theories on
medicine. His ideas on the nature of the cosmos—
namely that the order of the heavens was reflected in
the order of the body—carried over into medieval
times, when people believed that physical and
mental health was determined by the balance of
four specific fluids coursing throughout the body.
These fluids, called humors, from the Latin word
humor for "fluid," included blood, yellow bile, black
bile, and phlegm. Their mixture in different pro-
portions at different times was supposedly responsible for a person's overall disposition and for shifts
in mood. The person with a ruddy complexion was
supposedly full of warm blood and cheerful; he
therefore projected a sanguine outlook. The irasci-
ble, hot-tempered person had too much yellow bile,

The medieval humors

so his outlook became jaundiced and choleric. Too much black bile in the body caused the melancholy of a cold and sullen person, and the lazy, apathetic person's character was controlled by too much sluggish phlegm. It was believed that an excess of any one of these fluids not only altered one's temperament but also caused physical illness. Practitioners of health—one must refrain from calling them doctors—observed that during the course of an illness, there was an increase in the amount of fluids discharged from the body. Taking their cues from such natural phenomena, they encouraged further draining of these secretions as a means of restoring the body to health. Bloodletting, purges, emetics, and other techniques were employed to release whatever "bad" blood, urine, diarrhea, vomit, bile, sweat, mucus, or phlegm was thought to be putting the body out of balance and causing illness. Knowing when to stop draining the discharges was anybody's guess, for the practitioner relied not on accurate measures but on only his own "sense of humors" to judge when his patient reached the right proportion. The concept of balanced humors prevailed until the eighteenth century, when "humor" took on the figurative meaning of "mood." We now realize that our physical and mental outlook on life depends a great deal on how we cope with our fluctuating moods and that keeping them in control is not simply a question of regulating our body fluids. However, the person who takes himself less seriously and sees the lighter side of problems possesses the perspective we call a sense of humor.

Names to Call People

The person contemptuously called an *addlebrain* is thought to be a muddled, confused bungler whose head is comparable to a rotten egg. In ancient Greek an egg that did not hatch was called *ourion oon,* an aborted "wind-egg." In translating the term into Latin, the addlebrained lexicographer made the mistake of writing it as *ovum urinae,* an egg of urine, or a spoiled egg. In Middle English *adel* was the word for urine. The adel egg, therefore, was the one that would not develop into a chicken but would decompose in urine. Although the connection with urine may have been forgotten, the element of spoiling influenced Henry Fielding to write in *The Covent Garden Journal* (1732): "My muddy brain is addled like an egg." Benjamin Disraeli continued the image in 1880 by having Zenobia, a character in his *Endymion,* say, "Never mind Lord Waverly and such addle-brains."

ADDLEBRAIN

This common term is older than one might imagine. In 1549 a Biblical scholar named Miles Coverdale denounced a critic of his work *Erasmus* by calling him "a blockheade that hathe loste the judgemente of nature." Until the recent development of plastics, it was the custom for hats and wigs

BLOCKHEAD

to be stored on heads made of wood. No time was wasted in lifting the term to apply it to a stupid person who has as much intelligence as a block of wood.

BLUE BLOOD   Proud Spaniards who lived over two hundred years ago are responsible for this term. Castilians fiercely defended their racial aristocracy by pointing to their veins, which looked bluer under the fair skin that their ancestors had passed on to them than the veins beneath the darker skin of those people whose ancestors had mixed with Jews or dark-skinned Moors. *Blue blood,* or *sangre azul,* became their proof of noble birth, a means of identifying the presumed superior purebloods in a destructively discriminating society. Since this inbreeding led to such unforeseen liabilities as retardation, and because world commerce led to new contacts, the practice dissolved. Today the term "blue blood" applies to any socially prominent and usually wealthy member of the upper class, whatever the bloodline.

BOOTLEGGER   In the late 1800s, when liquor was prohibited in dry states such as Oklahoma and Kansas, *bootleggers* earned a good living by smuggling liquor to American Indians in flat bottles tucked into their high boots. The term received further notoriety in the 1920s during Prohibition, when distributors of contraband liquor plied their goods in quantities greater than what would fit into even the biggest boots. Since that time bootlegging has come to mean trading or smuggling anything illegal. In 1928 an article in *The Saturday Evening Post* reported that "Since 1924 an unknown number of Mexicans have been 'bootlegged' across the border."

Confiding one's innermost thoughts to a *bosom buddy,* a person whom one can trust to keep those secrets locked deep inside his own chest, is as reassuring today as it was in 1590, when the writer Robert Greene exclaimed in *Never Too Late,* "There is nothing better than a bosom friend with whom to conferre." In 1699 the Earl of Shaftesbury wrote of the joy of confessing "the secrets of the breast unfolded to a bosom-friend." At one point the term became a sardonic barb, conveying the untrustworthiness of a back-biter. Around 1732 a certain Thomas Fuller invented the proverb—quoted in G. L. Apperson's *English Proverbs* (1929)—" 'No friend like to a bosom-friend,' as the man said when he pulled out a louse." Of particular interest is the nineteenth-century garment called the "bosom-friend" that women wore to protect their bodies from the cold. An article entitled "An Inquiry Concerning Virtue" discussed the design of these chest guards in the 1838 *Workwoman's Guide:* "Some persons do not hollow out bosom-friends, but knit them square or oblong." By the late nineteenth century the phrase had regained its earlier positive connotation, which has persisted to the present day, as people in the armed forces helped to

BOSOM BUDDY

popularize the concept of a "bosom chum" or "bosom buddy."

BROWN-NOSER The most despicable sort of sycophant is the *brown-noser*. He is the toady whose only interest is in currying favor for his self-aggrandizement. While the apple-polisher often manages to disguise his intentions, thereby earning praise until his motives become obvious, the brown-noser lowers himself into the abject position of paying close attention to his superior's bottom. A fairly recent term, brown-noser—along with its synonyms "bum-sucker" and "ass-licker"—used to be a taboo word. Abbreviations like "a brownie" and "to brownie up" have removed the taint from the term and elevated it to relative respectability.

DUNDERHEAD This supposedly nonsensical term for a stupid, spiritless person is actually most meaningful and fitting. Whisky distilleries in Scotland were the source of the word "dunder," the name given to the overflow of liquors being fermented. The leftover sediment and froth contain little of the spirits that stay within the vat and give the finished product its potency. By easy transference, a person with a head full of dunder could be said to be just as vapid.

Egghead became an elitist term during the American presidential election of 1952. Although it was coined in the 1930s to describe a balding, vapid intellectual lacking any spark of interest in popular trends, supporters of the liberal-minded Democratic candidate Adlai Stevenson revived the term hoping to turn it to their own advantage. Because Stevenson's high forehead and receding hairline gave his head a definite oval shape, his supporters tried to turn this liability into an asset by calling themselves eggheads to indicate that they and their candidate were more forward-looking, politically advanced, and intelligent than the opposition. They succeeded in attracting the vote of the intelligentsia, although Stevenson did not win the election. His defeat undoubtedly helped to restore the term's previous connotation of "out of it," with its implication that intellectualism is more of a minus than a plus.

EGGHEAD

The man called a *heel* is considered as low as one can go. In the early 1900s, "heel" was an underworld term for a sneaky, petty thief. From the 1920s to the 1940s it identified an untrustworthy cad who abused women, and from the 1940s on, the name has stood both for that particularly disgusting person also known as a *brown-noser* (see page 128) who follows his superiors for favors and for the all-around low-down character who deserves to be trodden upon. "Heel" may be a shortened version

HEEL

of the seventeenth-century taboo word "shit-heel," which meant a persistent follower who was always at one's heels and whose presence underfoot could not go unnoticed.

HIGHBROW   The theory behind the origin of *highbrow,* or a person with intellectual tastes, was that a longer than usual distance from the ridge of one's nose to one's hairline, such that one's eyebrows also appeared higher than normal, indicated that the subject possessed a larger, more well-developed brain. A writer for the New York *Sun* named Will Irwin took credit for inventing the term around 1902 and using it in his articles to identify an intelligent, cultured lover of the arts and literature. (The opposite "lowbrow" was also his invention.) In *Ann Veronica* (1909), H. G. Wells used the term to characterize more than just a room by writing, "Their very furniture had mysteriously a high-browed quality." Contrary to his intentions, however, Mr. Irwin had coined a term that turned on itself, for it soon became applied not to a sincere, truly cultured individual but to one who consciously adopted an air of erudite superiority to elevate his image. Anti-intellectuals criticized the supercilious attitude of highbrows who would raise one *supercilium*—the Latin word for eyebrow—in a look of disdain. Even today the term retains its derogatory connotation.

The *hippie* of the 1960s earned his name not from a   HIPPIE
body part but from the 1920s jazz slang term "hep,"
which meant "in the know" and derived from
"Step!" or "Hep!" for "Keep in step!"—the military
drill command to soldiers or horses. The expression
"Get hep," which meant "Step lively," "Be on the
alert," and "Be the first to know," evolved into the
simple adjective "hip" during the progressive 1960s.
For, although hippies appeared to be blasé and un-
involved, their credo of dropping out from con-
ventional society was based on being tuned in, or
"hip" to, but consciously rejecting examples of
commercialism and materialism.

A perpetual condition, a characteristic of Little Boy   LAZYBONES
Blues since ancient times, the term has probably
been around in one form or another for just as long.
In 1600 Nicholas Breton wrote in *Pasquil's Madcap,*
"Go tell the Labourers, that the lazie bones that will
not worke must seeke the beggar's gaines." An unknown clever soul made a profit out of sloth in the
late 1700s, when he dubbed the instrument he originated "the lazybones." Resembling a long pair of
tongs, his short-lived invention enabled fat, lazy,
elderly, and infirm people to pick up things without
stooping. Comparable utensils today may serve similar functions but sadly lack such a fitting name.

LEATHERNECK   As a nickname for a U. S. Marine, *leatherneck* came into use only around 1830 even though the short, close-fitting coat having black leather sewn at the neck (black silk for officers) was adopted as a uniform in 1804 and was worn in the War of 1812. Navy men riled their military brothers by maintaining that sailors kept cleaner than Marines. They boasted of stripping to the waist to wash completely, while accusing Marines of washing only their arms, hands, and head, since their necks were always covered.

LONGHAIR   Like the aforementioned "egghead" and "high-brow," *longhair* is a term reserved for intellectuals, particularly those with sophisticated tastes in music. In the mid-1950s, in contrast with the popular trend toward short hair, men committed to the creative arts took to growing their hair longer, recalling famous predecessors such as Bach, Mozart, Beethoven, and Liszt, each of whom sported the longer hairstyle of his time. The convictions of twentieth-century longhairs stemmed more from their commitment to artistic individuality than from a need to make a statement of social protest against an established regime. Although the term initially described not only those who created difficult, esoteric music, but also those who appreciated it, "longhair" transcended its musical classification. Today a longhaired approach means having a serious, idealistic, and often impractical perspective conditioning one's entire outlook.

Calling a person a *muscleman* can be both a compliment and an insult. Certainly weight lifters, circus
strong men, and wrestlers would not take offense.
But the term was also an early-twentieth-century
underworld slang name for a thug who was hired to
use his strength for violence. His eagerness to move
in without compunction gave rise to the phrase *to
muscle in,* or to take advantage of another's better
circumstances by forcibly taking what one covets
for one's own profit. All of this hefty pushing and
shoving stems from a little mouse—the translation
of the Latin *musculus* and the root word for muscle—which appears to run back and forth under the
skin when a person flexes the muscles of his upper
arm.

MUSCLEMAN

Muscleman

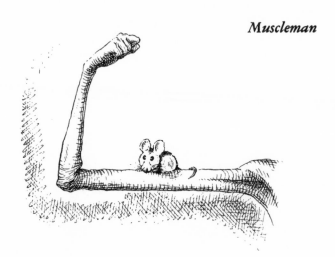

NOSEY PARKER *Nosey Parker* is a distinctively British epithet for an inquisitive busybody. The pest who earns this title is not easily discouraged. Having maneuvered himself so as to "park" his nose into another person's affairs, he intends to stay awhile. The etymologist Edwin Radford offers some interesting commentary in his *Unusual Words* (1946). He recounts the suggestion of Harold Wheeler, the author of *How Much Do You Know?*, that the original Nosey Parker was Matthew Parker (1504–1575), Anne Boleyn and Henry VIII's chaplain and later Elizabeth I's archbishop of Canterbury, who had both a long nose and a reputation for prying into others' business. Radford also retells the account Stanley Rogers wrote in *From Ships and Sailors* that the first Nosey Parker may have been a certain Richard Parker, renowned nosey person and the instigator of the Sheerness Mutiny, for which he was hanged from the yardarm of the H.M.S. *Sandwich* on June 30, 1797. Even if neither of these speculations is totally authentic, the word "nose" has been synonymous with "informer" for a long time, and "Parker" could be a corruption of the dialect word "pauk," to be inquisitive. In 1915 P. G. Wodehouse summed up the obstinacy of such a nuisance in *Something Fresh:* " 'But Nosey Parker is what I call him,' she said. 'He minds everybody's business as well as his own.' "

Redneck has both an American and South African background. A derogatory term for Southern white laborers from the mid-1800s, it came about as the logical result of their having to work long hours in the fields, their necks becoming burned and toughened under the sun. In 1938, during the Depression, a Southern editor named Jonathan Daniels tried to cleanse the term and restore pride to the rednecks' descendants by writing, "But a redneck is by no means to be confused with po' whites. Lincoln and Jackson came from a Southern folk the backs of whose necks were ridged and red from labor in the sun." Half a world away the Boers applied the Afrikaans name *rooinek* to uneducated British masses during the South African wars of the later 1800s. The term persisted as a means of insulting any British or European immigrant to South Africa.

REDNECK

Crowds have little patience with the innocent but annoying *rubbernecker,* who cranes his head and stretches his neck to see everything in sight. The word was coined around 1895 to describe an unsophisticated person who gawked naïvely in wide-eyed enchantment. As time went on, his fascination with the world became fuel for his critics, who labeled him "green" and a fool for his ingenuousness. His habit also led to revenues for the travel business. By the early 1900s, the term and its variation "rubberneck car" were nicknames for observation cars on

RUBBER NECKER

Rubbernecker

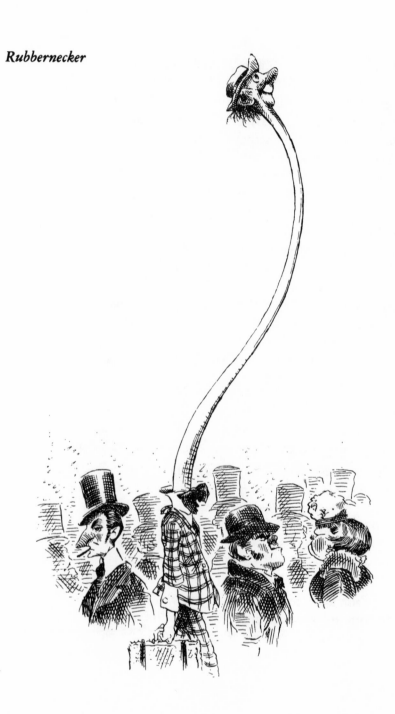

passenger trains and for sightseeing buses. In 1932 the British mystery writer Dorothy Sayers indicated the displeasure of one of her characters in *Have His Carcase:* "She . . . could not waste time rubbernecking around Wilvercombe with Lord Peter Wimsey." H. L. Mencken admired the term, writing with typical humor, "J.Y.P. Grieg, the Scots professor, was quite right when he described *rubberneck* as 'one of the best words ever coined.' It may be homely, but it is nevertheless superb, and whoever invented it, if he could be discovered, would be worthy not only of a Harvard LL.D. but also of the thanks of both Rotary and Congress, half a bushel of medals and thirty days as the husband of Miss America."

SKINFLINT

The stingy, nit-picking *skinflint* has been around since before the 1700s, when bits of flint were used to make a fire. The term resulted from comparing the person who pinched pennies with the one who tried to split rocks down to their thinnest layer or skin to eke out more flint for the fire. The epitome of a greedy person, the contemporary skinflint attempts to arrange every fine detail of a bargain down to the thinnest "skin" of flint, or to his exacting specifications. The next-to-nothing value of the skin of a flint can be equated with *lana caprina,* Latin for "goat wool," while the French phrase *tondre sur un oeuf* captures the worthlessness of something as thin as the lining of an eggshell.

TENDERFOOT   *Tenderfoot* has both American and British origins.
The term applied in seventeenth-century England
to horses that required breaking-in before they

Tenderfoot

could perform heavy tasks. Until recently the British used it as a derogatory term for vagrants on the lookout for a ride. The California Gold Rush of 1849 saw the emergence of the term in America. People who raced to the West in search of gold grew footsore from being unused to the physical hardships of pioneer life, one of which was traveling long distances by foot. Besides calling them tenderfeet, experienced Forty-Niners labeled them "raw-heels" because the new arrivals were not accustomed to wearing boots. Ranchers also applied the term "tenderfeet" to imported cattle. By extension, anyone who experiences difficulty in a new situation has tender feet. Immigrants were so called until they became initiated into the rigors of their new life and shed their "greenhorn" status. In 1900 Owen Wister described the tentative timidity of *The Virginian:* "In my tenderfoot innocence I was looking indoors for the washing arrangements."

TWO-FACED JANUS

A person called a *two-faced* or *two-headed Janus* is usually one who is thought to be dishonest to the point of being deceitful. The ancient Romans did not have treachery in mind when they worshiped their god Janus, the guardian of doors and gates, including the entrance to heaven, who kept watch over the beginnings of things. They even named the opening month of the year, January, in his honor. With two faces, one in front and one in back, Janus had the power to see both forward and backward at the same time. Because of his hindsight and fore-sight, the temple to him in the Roman Forum had not a single but a double arch with doors. The closing of both doors symbolized peace within the Roman Empire; leaving the doors open meant that Janus was being called upon to examine the past and future as a means of resolving wars being waged somewhere in the empire. By modern times the ro-mance of mythology had fallen as surely as the Roman Empire itself. "Janus-faced" earned its con-notation of unfairness and insincerity when people rejected the validity of looking both ways at once. In 1711 the third Earl of Shaftesbury, Anthony Ashley Cooper, criticized his contemporaries thus in *Characteristics of Men, Manners, Opinions:* "This Janus-faced of writers, who with one countenance force a smile, and with another show nothing beside rage and fury." A Janus-faced situation still is thought to be one with two sides to it.

There is one important, far-reaching qualification to the popular definition of Janus-faced as deceitful. Some more generous interpreters of the phrase hold that it could really mean quite the opposite of the currently held definition and thereby open up new avenues of thinking. They maintain that Janus is actually the symbol for open-mindedness, for by having two faces, indicating that there is more than one way of looking at things, he can examine all views and even accept opinions from opposing sides. Simultaneously reactionary and liberal, this philosophy, like the expectations of the ancient Romans, leaves room for a number of options. It invites both greater understanding and less arbitrary judgment of polarized issues. The American psychiatrist and social behaviorist Albert Rothenberg presents a convincing thesis in the November, 1979, issue of *Psychology Today* that creative people consciously conceive of natural contradictions and integrate them into original expressions of art, music, literature, and science. Preoccupation with the tension of contrasting ideas, or wrestling with the coexistence of what he calls "simultaneous antitheses," is the basis of the philosophy Rothenberg has termed "janusian thinking." The barb of being called a two- or more-faced Janus may therefore soon lose its sting and emerge as a coveted compliment for all exponents of the creative process.

Bibliography

Adams, J. Donald. *The Magic and Mystery of Words.* New York: Holt, Rinehart and Winston, 1963.

Andrews, William. *Old-Time Punishments.* London: The Tabard Press Ltd., 1890.

Armour, J.S. *The Genesis and Growth of English.* New York: Oxford University Press, 1935.

Barnett, Lincoln. *The Treasure of Our Tongue.* New York: Alfred A. Knopf, 1964.

Brewer, E. Cobham. *Dictionary of Phrase and Fable.* Philadelphia: Henry Altemus Co., 1898.

_____. *Brewer's Dictionary of Phrase and Fable,* revised by Ivor Evans. New York: Harper and Row, 1970.

Carothers, Gibson, and Lacey, James. *Slanguage.* New York: Sterling, 1979.

Chapman, Bruce. *Why Do We Say Such Things?* New York: Miles-Emmett, 1947.

Collins, V.H. *A Book of English Idioms.* Bristol, England: Longmans, Green, 1956.

_____. *A Second Book of English Idioms.* Bristol, England: Longmans, Green, 1958.

_____. *A Third Book of English Idioms.* Bristol, England: Longmans, Green, 1960.

_____. *A Book of English Proverbs.* Bristol, England: Longmans, Green, 1959.

Davies, T. Lewis. *A Supplementary English Glossary.* London: George Bell and Sons, 1881.

1811 Dictionary of the Vulgar Tongue, edited by Captain Francis Grose. Chicago: Follett, 1971 (originally compiled in 1796).

Eisiminger, Sterling. "Colorful Language," *Verbatim,* vol. VI, no.1, Summer 1979, pp.1-3.

Ernst, Margaret. *In a Word.* Great Neck, New York: Channel Press, 1939.

____. *More About Words.* New York: Knopf, 1968.

Evans, Bergen, and Evans, Cornelia. *A Dictionary of Contemporary American Usage.* New York: Random House, 1957.

Flexner, Stuart Berg. *I Hear America Talking.* New York: Simon and Schuster, 1976.

Frazer, Sir James G. *The Golden Bough,* abridged edition. New York, Macmillan, 1922.

Freeman, William. *A Concise Dictionary of English Idioms.* New York: Crowell, 1951.

Funk, Charles Earle. *A Hog on Ice.* New York: Harper and Brothers, 1948.

____. *Heavens to Betsy!* New York: Harper and Brothers, 1955.

____. *Thereby Hangs a Tale.* New York: Harper and Brothers, 1950.

____ and Funk, Charles Earle, Jr. *Horsefeathers.* New York: Harper and Brothers, 1958.

Funk, Wilfred. *Word Origins and Their Romantic Stories.* New York: Wilfred Funk, 1950.

Halliwell-Philips, James Orchard. 7th ed. *A Dictionary of Archaic and Provincial Words, Obsolete Phrases, Proverbs and Ancient Customs from the Fourteenth Century.* 2 vols. London: George Routledge and Sons, 1924.

Holt, Alfred H. *Phrase Origins.* New York: Crowell, 1936.

Jacobs, Noah Jonathan. *Naming-Day in Eden. New York: Macmillan, 1958.*

Mackay, Charles. *A Glossary of Obscure Words in the Writings of*

Shakespeare and his Contemporaries. London: Gilbert and Rivington, Ltd., 1887.

____. *The Lost Beauties of the English Language, an appeal to authors, poets, clergymen, and public speakers.* New York: Bouton, 1874.

Mencken, H.L. *The American Language.* New York: Knopf, 1937, and Supplement II, 1948.

Morris, William, and Morris, Mary. *Morris Dictionary of Phrase and Word Origins.* New York: Harper and Row, 1977.

Murray, James A.H.; Bradley, Henry; Craigie, W.A.; and Onions, C.T. *The Oxford English Dictionary.* 12 vols. Oxford: The Clarendon Press, 1933.

Nares, Robert. *A Glossary of Words, Phrases, Names, and Allusions in Works of English Authors, Particularly of Shakespeare and His Contemporaries.* London: George Routledge and Sons, 1905.

The Oxford English Dictionary. 12 vols. Oxford: Clarendon, 1933.

Partridge, Eric. *A Dictionary of Catch Phrases.* New York: Stein and Day, 1977.

____. *Dictionary of Clichés.* New York: Macmillan, 1940.

Radford, Edwin. *Unusual Words and How They Came About.* New York: Philosophical Library, 1946.

____, and Radford, Mona A. *Encyclopedia of Superstitions,* edited and revised by Christina Hole. London: Hutchinson, 1961.

Reid, Alastair. *Ounce, Dice, Thrice.* Boston: Little, Brown, & Co., 1958.

Schwartz, Alvin. *Cross Your Fingers, Spit in Your Hat.* Philadelphia: Lippincott, 1974.

Shipley, Joseph T. *Dictionary of Early English.* New York: Philosophical Library, 1955.

Skeat, Walter William. *A Glossary of Tudor and Stuart Words, especially from the dramatists.* Oxford: The Clarendon Press, 1914.

Standard Dictionary of Folklore, Mythology, and Legend, edited by Maria Leach. New York: Funk & Wagnalls, 1972.

Toone, William. *A Glossary and Etymological Dictionary of Obsolete and Uncommon Words.* London: Wm. Pickering, 1832.

Webster's New World Dictionary, second college edition. New York: World, 1972.

Wentworth, Harold, and Flexner, Stuart Berg. *Dictionary of American Slang.* New York: Crowell, 1975.

Wright, Thomas. *Dictionary of Obsolete and Provincal English.* 2 vols. London: Henry G. Bohn, 1857.